A SHORT
HISTORY OF
SEVILLE

A SHORT HISTORY OF
SEVILLE

Rafael Sánchez Mantero

© SILEX® 1992
I.S.B.N.: 84-7737-039-7
Depósito Legal: M. 6.625-1992
Original tittle: Historia Breve de Sevilla
Translated by: Martin Smith
Cover and production: Sílex Ediciones
Planimetry: José Luis Guerrero Cela
Photocomposition: CTE, S.A.
Photoreproduction: Cromoarte, S.L.
Printed in Spain by: Gráficas Monterreina, S. A.

CONTENTS

FOREWORD

Seville is complex and deceptive city. At first sight it may appear lively, open and festive, but these characteristics relate to a more superficial level. A certain bitterness –the product of disillusions and frustrations suffered over the years– and an undeniable tendancy to vanity are other aspects that make up its collective personality.

Discovering the essence of Seville is not only a difficult task for the first time visitor; many people from Seville know very little about their own city.

A knowledge of the Seville of yesterday will surely provide some of the clues to the city as we find it today. Cities, like people, are marked by what they have lived through, by the influences they have received, by their days of happiness and glory and by their days of suffering and crisis. Seville has a rich history. Founded in the distant past, it had already gone through many changes before reaching its moment of splendour at the turn of the eighteenth century. But from this point on the decline set in, slowly but surely, the effect of which was to make Seville to cling too closely to its past.

The reader will find here a brief history of Seville. There is little room for detail and even less for erudition. The object of the work is to set before the reader the key events in that history, in an easy and accessible style without, however, a lack of rigour.

I hope the author, a contemporary historian, will be forgiven for the academic sin of offering a few chapters on Seville's remote past. It is hoped the evennes in treatment of the city's history viewed from the watchtower of the present, will make up for any disadvantages. In any case, it is for the reader to decide whether the objective has been achieved.

CHAPTER I

THE SEVILLE OF ARGANTONIO

The Origins of Seville

In the calle Mármoles, almost on the corner of the calle Aire, stand three large columns, the remains of a Roman temple dating back to the second century. Although they are the oldest architectural relics to be found in the city, Seville is, in fact, much older than that.

It is not easy, however, to determine the birth of Seville as a city with any exactitude. The mystery surrounding its origins has given rise to numerous legends and stories, each one attempting to explain it. One of the best known tells how Hercules came to these lands to avenge the death of his father, Osiris, murdered by his brother Tyfon, an ally of the three headed Gerion, then king of Spain. Hercules, after slaying Gerion, became entranced with the fertility and richness of the region and founded a city on the banks of its main river.

But legends are one thing and reality is another. In those primitive times the land on both banks of the river Guadalquivir, on which the city presently stands, was to all intents and purposes uninhabitable. The flooding of the river's banks left the land waterlogged for the best part of the year. Archeologists have discovered that while human remains on the highlands above the valley reach as far back as 300,000 years, there is little evidence that early inhabitants were in much of a hurry to go down to the river. Flooding must surely have presented enormous problems for would-be settlers. Only in the summer months would the hill people dare to set up encampments in the valley for the vigilance of their grazing beasts.

According to Saint Isidore and others, Seville's former name *Hispalis* bears a direct relation to the living conditions of the first inhabitants of the city. When some of the river's tributaries started drying out and early settlers chose land close to the river banks, they had to build their houses on wooden stilts to protect themselves from the rising waters. The settlement thus acquired the name *Hispalis*, or *island on stilts*.

One theory attempting to shed light on Seville's former name holds that it was the *Espalos*, the people of Escilia who accompanied Hercules on his journey, who gave the name *Espalis* or *Ispalis* to the city that he founded. Another links *Hispalis* with *Hispal*, the name of the river on which the city was built.

The weight of scholarly opinion, however, would appear to coincide on the fact that *Hispalis* is simply a derivation of the Latin *Hispania*.

The Mystery of the Tartessos

The origins of Seville are closely related to the Tartessan civilization. Historians are still at pains to clear up the mystery surrounding Tartessos. What was the origin of this people? How far did its dominion extend? Where was its capital situated?

First accounts of Tartessos come from classical sources and interpretations of these have stirred up a long controversy over the siting of the mythical city. Greek authors refer to Tartessos as an Iberian city. They also mention a river which was subsequently called Baitis. The Roman scholar, Rufo Festo Avieno, in a work entitled *Ora Maritima*, which includes data taken from the most ancient sources, identifies the name Tartessos with certain geographical formations in a territory which roughly corresponds with that of Andalusia today.

Tartessos has always been linked to fabulous riches and a highly developed civilization. Judging by the earliest accounts of

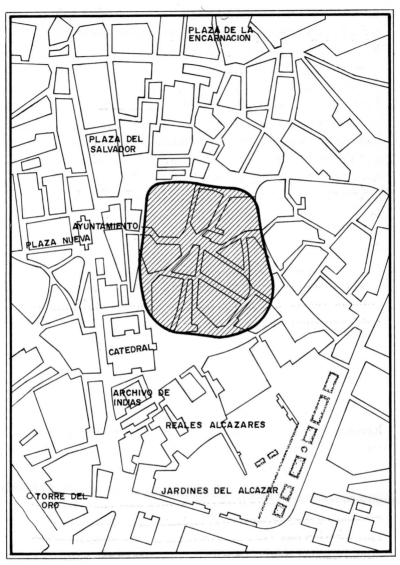

First inhabited settlements in Seville.

mythical city of Tartessos, it should not surprise us that Andalusia has long been linked with the *Garden of Eden*.

Cadiz, the island of Saltes in Huelva, and other places have been listed as possible sites of the capital of this kingdom. The lecturer Juan de Mato Carriazo was a staunch supporter of the theory that Tartessos was actually located in Sevilla. Perhaps the fact that it was he who discovered some of the few archeological artefacts of this ancient civilization to be unearthed to date goes some way to explaining his position. His most important find was, without doubt, the El Carambolo treasure, which is currently preserved in the Seville Ayuntamiento (Town hall), a replica of which can be viewed in the city's Archeological Museum.

The El Carambolo treasure was discovered in 1958 when excavations were carried out for the extension to the Tiro de Pichon, in the so-called El Carambolo hill, near Castilleja de la Cuesta. It comprises twenty one pieces of gold weighing three kilos in total. The pieces can be divided into two groups. The first is made up two bracelets, eight rectangular plates and a breastplate; the other by a breastplate, eight rectangular plates and an ornamental chain. The jewels were kept in earthenware vases at the back of a primitive hut, in a place experts consider must have been dedicated to worship. They were clearly not jewels for the everyday use of some dignitary but more likely were worn by men and women for specific ceremonies.

Studies to determine the age of the treasure date it at around 600 BC, and one expert has found a clear connection between these jewels and others found in the Eastern Mediterranean, particularily in Cyprus. This would seem to offer further evidence of Oriental, particularily Phoenician influences on the Tartessans, the first colonizers of our region.

The Tartessans, the oldest inhabitants of Sevilla, formed part of of the Iberian people who occupied a large part of the peninsula. This south western region was able to develop more than other regions thanks to agricultural and mineral riches and to Oriental and African influences.

The Colonizations

The Phoenicians were the first to be attracted by the riches of these lands and by about 700 BC had begun to penetrate into the Andalusian interior. Originally from the narrow coastal strip bound by the Lebanese mountains, they were pushed further out into the Mediterranean under pressure from Mesopotania and Egypt. They thus became merchants and seamen and their ships were eventually to drop anchor along the southern coasts of the Iberian Peninsula in search of the region's abundance of minerals.

Tradition has it that the Phoenicians founded the city of Cadiz in 1,100 BC, though there is no archeological evidence to support this. We do know, however, that they did not reach Seville until the eighth century. They settled here, in the first instance, due to the difficulties of navigation upriver from Seville. They saw in Seville an ideal base for trade with the entire region at the same time as being attracted by fabulous treasures it held.

Henceforth, the Guadalquiver river became a trade route and was to figure hugely in the Seville of the future. Rather than impeding the settling of its banks, it would actually encourage new settlers to the city.

The influence of the colonizers was soon to make itself felt. The Phoenicians enlarged the primitive settlement and built walls to protect both people and merchandise. They erected a wall on the banks of the river Tagarete which skirted the town to the south to act as a flood break, and built on the higher ground, safe from the vagaries of the river.

The city then occupied the space between what are now the Jardines de Murillo (Murillo gardens) and la plaza del Salvador. Seville became the trading centre for the whole region and people came from far and wide to attend its fairs and markets.

The Tartesian people benefited both materially and spiritually from the highly civilized Phoenicians who brought with them knowledge about mining techniques, building skills, the manufacture of textiles and dyes, and an alphabet which would serve as the basis for Iberian writing. They also brought thier own divinities.

In the Seville Architectural Museum there is a small, seated bronze statue of a naked goddess. A phoenician inscription at the base of the statue identifies it as the goddess of love and fertility *Astarte.* It was discovered in the outskirts of Seville and is from the seventh century BC. Another divinity brought by the Phoenicians, *Anat*, is also represented in a small figure in the same museum. Three small statues of the warlike god, *Reshef*, have been moved from Seville to the National Archeological Museum in Madrid.

The high point of Tartesian culture, the culmination of native riches and Oriental refinements brought by Phoenician colonizers, took place around the year 600 B.C.

The kingdom of the long-reigning Argantonio dates from between 630 and 555 BC. It was in one of those years that the Greek merchant, Kolaios de Samos, reached these shores after being pushed by winds from the Levant. He was warmly welcomed by Argantonio, who presumably wished to develop relations with Hellenic traders in order to avoid depending exclusively on the Phoenicians. Furthermore, the Greeks were accomplished sailors and experts in naval warfare. Kolais de Samos returned to his native country with a goodly quantity of silver coins and an offer from the king of Tartessos to allow those Greek families forced out by the Carthaginian advances to settle in his lands. However, they only accepted money to fortify their walls –which was not to stop them later getting pushed in.

The Greeks suffered a terrible defeat at the hands of the Carthaginians at the battle of Alalia in 533 AD. This battle clearly signalled the rise of Carthage. The Greeks were to continue trading with the Western Mediterranean, and relics of Greek ceramics from Seville and the surrounding area bear testimony to that. Amphoras, chandiliers and vases decorated with black and red figures dating from the end of the sixth century attest to the prescence of Greek influences during this period.

The Turdetan Era

The kingdom of Tartessos, without Greek aid, began to decline. While data relating to the end of the Tartesians is scant, historians consider the Turdetan era, lasting from the fifth century BC to the Roman conquest, as basically a degredation of the former one.

It was in this period that the south began to show marked differences from the rest of the peninsula.

Seville must have grown considerably throughout this epoch, but its continued expansion over successive eras from the original nucleus around the Cuesta del Rosario, calle Abades, Mateos Gago etc., has hampered archeological efforts to discover the extent of this growth. Four decades ago archeologists took advantage of building works being carried out in the Cuesta del Rosario to investigate the subsoil, and an assortment of articles including vessels and coins were unearthed as well as the remnants of a house from the Turdetan era. From the remains of the stone walls reinforced by mud and mortar we can imagine how the house must have looked. It would have been square shaped with three or four rooms tiled with irregular shaped slabs, clearly insufficinet to keep out the damp.

As Seville continued to be the exporting centre for the produce of the region, it was to be expected that it would grow towards the river, its trade route. Exports were chiefly precious metals, but also agricultural produce and esparto, flax and wool. Seville also served as port and distribution centre for imports from other areas.

The peaceful development which characterized the Turdetan era and the good relations enjoyed with the Phoenicians finally came to an end. For some still unknown reason the Turdetans tried to expel the Phoenicians who called to the Carthaginians for help.

The Carthaginian people, like the Phoenicians, originated from the Lebanon but had spread out over the eastern part of the Mediterranean. Their expansionist fever carried them westward to the southern part of the Iberian Peninsula.

Carthaginian control over Seville began around the middle of the IV century BC. A treaty with Rome signed in 348 BC is evidence of the fact that the Iberian Peninsula was now under Punic influence.

The conquest of the Turdetan region was initiated by Amilcar Barca, his son-in-law Asdrubal and his son Hannibal. After conquering Cadiz in the year 237 BC, they penetrated into the Guadalquivir valley there to confront the Turdetan leaders, Istolacio and Indortes. Seven years of war finally brought the Turdetans under Carthaginian rule. In the course of the war, the Carthaginians built the Carmona fortress, the remains of which make up the oldest example of military construction in the Peninsula.

Seville continued to prosper during the era of Carthaginian rule and its inhabitants lived very much as they had done in years gone by. The people of Seville, even then, were notable for their ability to assimilate foreign invasions, and make full use of the advantages which contact with other cultures and civilizations brought.

The outbreak of war between Carthage and Rome was soon to shatter this peace. A Turdetan rising, timed to coincide with the resulting Carthaginian military weakness, was quelled by Asdrubal. Many houses were razed to the ground and Seville lost part of its population in the fighting.

The arrival of the Romans to what they were to call la Betica would close the first and lengthy chapter in the history of Seville.

CHAPTER II

IULIA ROMULA HISPALIS

The Arrival of the Romans

The Roman arrival in the Iberian Peninsula and specifically in Seville was to signify a new and significant phase in the history of both peoples.

Rome proved to be one of the most decisive influences in the cultural and spiritual make-up of Seville, and in the city as it stands today we can still see vestiges of its presence. Some rather confused observers consider the Arabs to have been almost completely responsible for the definition of the cultural personality of the region, as if somehow forgetting the contribution of the Romans.

It would seem that at first the Romans had no intention of settling in the south of the Peninsula. They came to do battle with their enemies, the Carthaginians, and on completion of their mission fully intended to return. But as had happened in the past to other visitors and was to happen again in the future, they did not find it easy to leave this land of riches and these welcoming people. In other parts of the Peninsula the populace had risen up against the conquerer, but the city of Hispalis submitted graciously to this new power which promised to bring progress and development in its wake.

Italica was the first city to be built by the Romans. It was initially designed to house the veterans of the war with the Carthaginians and was built after the battle of Ilipa (Alcala del Rio) in

206 BC. Italica, due to its privileged position on high ground looking out over the river Guadalquivir and the character of its inhabitants, became a type of residential suburb of Seville.

Although few Romans actually settled in Hispalis, the city continued to thrive both commercially and with regard to its activities as a port. It stood to benefit from being part of a vast empire where commercial interchanges were on a grand scale.

Although the Roman conquest did not pose great problems for Seville, the civil wars and internal strife that were to emerge in Rome did have important repercussions.

The civil war between Mario and Sila was no more than a example of the general crisis of how to incorporate the new territories now under Roman rule. The war reached Seville between 91 BC and 89 BC. Quinto Sertorio, who had been tribune for the soldiers in the Betica region, was exiled from Rome by Sila. He sought refuge here and led a rising against Sila with the aim of gaining independance from Rome. The Roman Senate responded with a series measures to subdue the Sertorians which culminated in the battle fought in the fertile valley of Triana. The Roman troops defeated the Hispalians and severely punished them for their rebelliousness.

A few years later a further civil war broke out in the struggle for power between Caesar and Pompey.

Caesar and Seville

Caesar first set foot in Seville in 69 BC as quaestor to the orders of the governor of the lower part of Hispania.

He returned to Seville in the year 61 BC as praetor or governor of the province. His policies were politically favourable for the city and won him the respect and admiration of the natives.

When the new civil war broke out Caesar chose Spain as the setting for his battle with Pompey –it was here where the bulk of his forces were located– and Seville, not forgetful of the benefits and fiscal exemptions it had enjoyed under its ex-governor, rallied to him.

One whole legion of Pompey's troops deserted their general,

Marco Terencio Varron, and holed up in Seville, there to receive a warm welcome from the people of the city who provided them with food and lodging. The desertion acted like a lightning bolt and Pompey's troops fell into disarray. Varron, faced with such a situation, opted to take his own life.

The fact that Seville played an important role in Caesar's rise to power was not something the future emperor would forget. Once the Pompey problem had been resolved he returned to Rome in the year 49.

Caesar, however, made the mistake of leaving the province in the hands of the grossly inefficient Q. Casio Longinos. When Pompey's sons gathered together an army to confront Caesar, the people of Seville, tired of the practices of their governor, joined sides against him. Caesar was forced to return to Betica in what was to be his last military campaign, culminating in the battle of Munda, near Osuna, on March 17th 45 BC.

After the victory, Caesar came to Sevilla for the last time. He had a long-standing affection for the city. Many Sevillians though, blamed him for the bad administration they had had to live under during the previous years. The most radical elements, in a bid to stop Caesar setting foot in Hispalis, asked for support from Lusitanian rebels who crept stealthily into the city and slaughtered Caesar's advance detachment to the man. Caesar, meanwhile, encamped on the outskirts, refused to mount a direct attack on the city for fear of damaging or destroying it. In this he demonstrated the respect in which he held his beloved Seville. The Lusitanians, after setting fire to several ships moored at the riverside, left the city enclave and began their retreat. Caesar's legions caught up with them and decimated them.

Caesar died shortly afterwards but not before again showing his affection for Seville. In the same year (45 BC) he conferred special status on the city through which the Seville people became Roman citizens with full rights. The new *Colonia Iulia Rómulo Hispalis*, as he himself named it, opted for a political administration similar to the Roman one.

Seville, Mirror of Rome

The city of Seville was bounded by a network of walls of which there is no trace left today. To the north, the Roman wall ran between what is now Santa Catalina and the calle Alhondiga. To the east it followed a line from the calle Cuna through el Salvador to the cathedral and the Alcazar. To the west, it extended from los Jardines del Murillo to the Puerta de Carmona.

The centre of this enclosure was situated in what is now the plaza de la Alfalfa. The Decumana Mayor, one of the main streets of the city, ran from here to the Puerta de Carmona. Water, reaching Seville from the other side of the city wall, was transported by an aqueduct, some of whose arches still remain. The other axis of the city was formed by the Cardo Maximo, which ran from Santa Catalina, through the Alfalfa, and on to the Cathedral.

The forum or nerve centre of the metropolis was located at the confluence of these two streets. Official buildings sprang up around them adding to the hive of constructional activity going on in the city. Three columns of a second century temple still stand in the calle Marmoles. Two others were moved to the Alameda de Hercules in 1574, and a sixth fell apart during removal to the Alcazar.

An important civil building must have stood in El Salvador on ground later occupied by a large mosque in the Arab period, and still later by a Christian temple.

For a city with such thriving commercial activity and to which flowed such considerable riches, it comes as no surprise that there were two huge hot baths. One was situated close to the forum and the other a little further south, near a mercantile centre which was later built near the cathedral. Recent excavations have uncovered remains of the latter baths which confirm their significant size.

The port of Seville exported produce from all over the region to the capital of the Roman Empire. Vegetable oil, wheat, minerals and other products were loaded on ships moored on the banks of the Guadalquiver, bound for Rome and other places. The intense dockside activity brought work to the shipyards.

Tall ships were built here and repairs were carried out to the hulls and sails of the boats which plied the river Betis.

Although no traces of buildings dedicated to public spectacleshave been uncovered, we can safely assume that a theatre oramphitheatre existed outside the city walls.

That very little remains of the majestic Seville of the Roman era was lamented by the eighteenth century Sevillian poet and scholar Rodrigo Caro when he wrote: "Although in Seville there were sumptuous and imposing temples, circuses, theatres and amphitheatres, statues and other public and private ornaments, everything has disappeared. The inundations of the river, the invasions of the Goths, Silnigos and Vandals, and most recently the Mohammedan Barbarians, have tarnished them".

While urbanistically and monumentally Seville was taking on a distinctly Roman look, other aspects of cultural and administrative life were also being Romanized. The adoption of Latin over the vernacular language was an important part of this process and had become generalized by the beginning of this Era. But the use of Latin in Seville did not exclude other languages –Greek for example– which was spoken amongst certain sectors of the population. It was to be expected that in a city based on commerce, and to which came people from the Eastern Mediterranean, this language would be spoken.

A predominantly land-owning aristocracy began to develop in Seville, beneficiaries of Caesar's redistribution of lands following the termination of the civil wars. This aristocracy took over public positions, the most important of which were the *Dunviros*. In effect, the dunviros were the equivalent of mayors, and it was decided that in order to avoid corruption and for one to control the other, there should be two. They had administrative, military and even religious functions.

The aediles were other public officers who had police and vigilance duties. The quaestors were responsible for the public treasury.

In 27 BC, during Augustus' period, Hispalis was made capital of Betica, one of the three provinces into which the Iberian Peninsula had been divided. Hispalis was thus capital of the *convent* or administrative district which extended further than the boundaries of the Seville province of today, taking in Huelva and parts of Badajoz.

A period of great tranquility followed. Hispanic people began to have increasing influence in Rome, culminating in the election of two emperors born in Italica, Seville: Trajan and Hadrian.

Seville's Emperors

Marco Ulpio Trajan, born in Italica in the year 53 AD, was Emperor of Rome from 98 to 117 AD. His father, Trajan the elder, was one of the Spaniards who had made his political career in Rome. He had been governor of Syria and Asia, proconsul of Betica (Andalusia) and consul during Vespasian's era. His son Trajan began his military career and was soon appointed consul by Domitian, and later governor of Upper Germany. On the death of Nerva he was proclaimed emperor. His greatest achievment was the extension of the empire's frontiers to include Rumania as well as Mesopotamia and Armenia.

Curiously, the majority of Sevillian celebrities appear consecutively and this was to be no exception; the emperor Hadrian took over after Trajan.

Hadrian, Trajan's nephew, was born in the year 76 and was Roman emperor from 117 to 138 AD. He was more intellectual than his uncle, who had taken over guardianship of him on his father's death. His reign was characterized by the rejection of expansionist policies in favour of the consolidation of existing frontiers and the search for peace. He was a tireless traveller and one of the Empire's most energetic exponents of public works and the construction of monuments.

Italica, Hadrian's birthplace, for years home to an excellent bust of the Emperor before it was moved to its current location in Seville's Archeological Museum, benefited from his interest in urban reforms. He extended the city by building what he called the *nova urbs*, –precisely the part which has survived to the

Bust of the Italian born Emperor Trajan.

present day. The rest, the oldest part, lies buried beneath the village of Santiponce.

Overall, Italica is the best conserved city in the peninsula. For centuries, however, it lay in ruins. Neglect, lack of interest, and the questionable scruples of some Sevillians resulted in stones being used for new buildings, and mosaics and statues carried off to adorn private mansions.

Italica's location in the Aljarafe hills dominating the Guadalquiver river and only two hours walking distance from Seville, gave it a privileged position from its inception.

For the great historian and archeologist Blanco Freijeiro, the urban layout and the width of the streets are more reminiscent of Oriental than western cities. It was surrounded by a wall of which only the remains stand today. The houses, though not great in number, were large and ornate and the majority had two stories, patios, mosaics and abundant water. The largest, known as the Casa de la Exedra, occupies an entire block. Perhaps the best known is the Casa de los Pajaros (House of the Birds) for its unusual and well preserved central mosaic in which various species of birds can be clearly distinguished.

The most spectacular building and the one which shows most clearly the importance of the city during its days of greatest splendour is the amphitheatre. With a length of 160 metres, a width of 130 metres and a capacity for 25,000 spectators, it was one of largest enclosures for public spectacles in the Roman world. In addition to the tiers, the lowest of which are still preserved, the amphitheatre has a rectangular cavity in the sand, of some three metres in depth, which served as dressing rooms or to house the cages of the animals taking part in the events.

Italica also had two theatres, the most important of which has been recently excavated.

The abundance and capacity of buildings for public spectacles might seem surprising given the low and select population of the city. But this would surely have been the site for celebrations lasting several days, whether for purposes of elections or religious or other events, attracting visitors from the entire region. Once in Italica they would stay to enjoy the celebrations and fill the tiers of the theatres and amphitheatres until the very last moment.

Italica had a perfect sewage system, still visible today, which gives us an idea of the level of development and comfort enjoyed by its inhabitants. The statues from its houses, streets and temples, now preserved in the Archeological Museum of Sevilla, are evidence to the richness of the city. The most impressive are of the god *Mercury*, *Jupiter's* messenger and protector of commerce; *Diana*, the goddess of Latin origin who corresponds to the Greek *Artemis*, dressed in a short tunic and surely carrying in her right hand (which has regrettably been lost) a bow for hunting; and lastly Apollo, her twin brother, and god of the Arts.

From the end of the second century, the Roman Empire began to suffer from a series of conflicts provoking social and economic crisis. The south of the Iberian peninsula became the object of frequent attacks and raids by the Mauritanians. The *VII Gemina Legion* was posted to Italica during the reign of Marco Aurelio for the defence of the city.

In spite of all the difficulties experienced during the third century, Hispalis had become the single most important city in Hispania, not only as the commercial centre of a rich region, but also because the adminstrative reforms of Diocletian had converted it into the centre of the five peninsular provinces and the two dependant ones, and because the viceregent of the Hispanic Diocese took up residence here.

At the point when the Roman Empire began its decline, Seville had become the first city in Spain and the eleventh in the world.

CHAPTER III

THE SEVILLA OF
SAINTS LEANDRO AND ISIDORE

The introduction of Christianity to Seville

The impression left by the splendour of the Roman era was to last for centuries, but already by the end of the third century new elements were coming into play which were to further shape its historical personality. Christianity was, without doubt, one of the most decisive of those elements.

Though some historians claim that Christianity arrived in Spain directly from Rome, the most accepted contemporary theory holds that it was brought in from the North of Africa. It was propagated by Spanish soldiers in the Roman army who carried out various missions there, as well as by traders calling frequently at places in the south of the Peninsula.

First accounts of the organization of the Church in Seville centre around Bishop Marcelo, the governor of this diocese from 250 to 280. The Church in Spain was organized according to the administrative regions drawn up by Diocletian and divided into five ecclesiastic regions, Seville becoming the headquarters of the Betica province.

While no archeological remains exist to testify to the presence and diffusion of Christianity in Seville, there are literary texts which substantiate it. The Romans persecuted the Christians for having beliefs that undermined the bases of their social structure –both master and slave had the right to salvation, and they were opposed to the cult of the emperor and worship of Pagan dieties.

The persecution of Christians in Seville created martyrs, among the most famous of which were the Saints Justa and Rufina. The idealized image of these saints was captured forever by Murillo in a famous painting presently kept in Seville's Museum of Art.

Justa and Rufina were potters who went daily to the city's market to sell their earthenware pots. One day in July, when the Pagan world celebrated the resurrection of Adonis, a group from a procession carrying the Syrian god Salambo stopped to ask the two women for a donation. This they refused angrily, maintaining that they worshipped the Christian God and not a Pagan idol. In the ensuing quarrel many of the pots and vases were smashed to pieces. Incensed by this, Justa and Rufina managed to knock the idol off its platform.

The irate potters were apprehended by security agents and tried and condemned for the sacrilege they had committed. The city's governor, Diogenes, ordered them to be put to death. Rufina was duly burned in the amphitheatre and Justa, after meeting her death in prison, had her body unceremoniously thrown into a well. Bishop Sabino, Marcelo's successor, managed to have her body removed from there and buried, together with her friend, in a cemetery which is today the site of the new railway station –called Santa Justa.

In homage to the first Christian martyrs in Seville, Justa and Rufina were named patrons of the city and raised to sainthood by the Church. Their fame spread far beyond the city's boundaries. Basilicas were built in their honour in Alcala de los Gazules and Vejer de la Frontera, in the province of Cadiz. Other Christians, notably the deacon Felix and Geroncio in Italica, followed them into martyrdom.

The year 313 was to mark the end of the persecutions, when Emperor Constantine promulgated the Edict of Milan. With the conversion of the Emperor Theodosius to Christianity in the year 380, the Christian community enjoyed a spectacular growth in numbers.

During those years a basilica was built over the remains of

San Vicente Martir which had arrived to Seville from Valencia. Though its exact location is still not clear, relics dicovered in the Patio de Banderas in the Alcazar have led to conjecture that it may have been located here.

Although few archeological remains are preserved of the early Christians, a representation of the Good Shepherd can still be seen in the Casa de Pilato, together with some stone coffins. The most interesting of these was discovered in la Iglesia de San Sebastian. For many years it had inadvertently been used as a bench in the church gardens.

The Barbarian Invasion

From the Constantine era onwards, pressure from North Europe began to sap the strength of the Roman Empire. When the Swabians, Vandals and Alani began invading the peninsula in 409, exhausted and demoralized Roman soldiers could do little to stop them.

The Siling Vandals, who arrived in Seville in the year 426, occupied the rich latifundiums and sacked and pillaged at will. It is said that their king Gunderic, after desecrating the San Vicente Martir church, received his divine punishment by being struck down dead on its porch. The Vandals soon went on to Africa leaving little of note in these lands –not even the name Andalusia as was once claimed. Their place was taken by the Swabians whose stay was also short-lived.

After the middle of the V century things began to quieten down. After years of invasions and continual change, Seville was in a state of crisis. Although little has been documented regarding this period, we do know that the city was in a state of paralysis with a scarcity of food and a general atmosphere of sadness and melancholy very much in contrast to the times of Roman splendour. Everything had changed, even down to the clothes people wore. Whilst the women adorned their hair with ornate headgear, the men usually wore theirs short with a fringe, somewhat in the style of monks. Examples of togas worn in this period show them to be more austere and supported by a clasp or brooch on the right shoulder.

The Visigoths, however, were to more profoundly affect the development of Hispalis. When the first Barbarian invaders left, Seville once again came under the decadent control of Rome, now lacking an organization to control its dominions and bereft of the power to hold on to its posessions. Nevertheless, it continued to burden the populace with increasingly unpopular taxes. The population of Seville was mainly Hispanic-Roman with various minority groups of which the Jewish community was the most numerous, occupying a whole area of the city.

When the Visigoths reached the Betica region in the first half of the fifth century they were generally well received. In Seville some of them married into rich landowning families. A case in point is Teudis, who was to reign in Spain between 539 and 548, and who set up court here. A Visigoth palace was built in the grounds of what is now the Iglesia del Salvador. Teudis was assassiated in this palace as was his successor Teudiselo, tragically cut down in the midst of celebrating a banquet.

The Visigoth court was moved to Merida in mid-century during Agila's reign, and later to Toledo under Atanagild.

Hermengild's uprising against his father, King Leovigildo proved to be the most noteworthy event in Seville under the Visigoths. Hermengild was appointed governor of Betica province and set up home in Seville. Here, his French and catholic wife Ingundis, with the help of Saint Leandro, converted him to Catholicism. His baptism was an act of rebellion against his father who held to the Arian religion. Hermengildo crowned himself king in 579 and began to mint money. Leovigild chose not to intervene immediately but, instead, waited three years before taking action to crush the rebellion. From a base in Italica he laid siege to Seville, cut of the supply of water and food, and waited until Hermengild had no option but to surrender.

Leovigild, having, in this instance, acted wisely, decided to banish and imprison his own son. Hermengild was later assassinated in Tarragona in circumstances still far from clear.

The Bishop of Seville, Leandro, played an important role throughout Hermengild's rebellion. Born in Cartagena into an influential Hispanic-Roman family –his father a top civil servant in the administration who had taken refuge in Seville in 554 from the Byzantines who had then occupied that part of the Levant. Here, Leandro embarked on his ecclesiastical career, became a monk, and in time was appointed bishop. In this position he was able to give assistance to Hermengild in his campaign against his father, even travelling to Constantinople to summon up help. The two years he spent there were to give him a deep insight into the classical Greek-Latin culture and inspire him to conceive the idea of a huge cultural centre in Seville. On his return he was exiled by Leogivild, although, curiously, the same king would later entrust the education of Ricared, his other son, to Leandro. He was the organizer of the III Council of Toledo in 589, a year before his death.

Leandro was succeded by his younger brother Isidore. The new bishop, born in 560, would later be raised to sainthood like his brother before him. Leandro had a strong influence on him and played a decisive part in his education. Saint Isidore's intellectual work was impressive and it was as a result of his efforts that Seville became one of the most important cultural centres of its time. The ecclesiastical college in Seville was founded by Leandro but Isidore further improved it by adding an extensive library of religious and scientific books. Its prestige was such that scholars the world over came to study here.

Saint Isidore published various works, the most important of which are *The Etymologies*, a type of encyclopedia of the knowledge of the time, and the *Chronicon*, a treatise on universal history.

Although he has been considered as a mere librarian of knowledge with little original input of his own, he should be given credit for having been able to adapt that knowledge to his time, and to have blended his own wisdom with that of others. What cannot be denied, however, is the extent of Isidore of Seville's influence on Medieval Europe.

His work in both the political and strictly religious areas was notable. He worked laboriously to spread the idea of a state formed by a new society in which a Hispanic-Roman substratum would be integrated with a Gothic element. He was advisor to the Kings Gundemar, Sisebut, Swintil and Sisenand, as well as promotor of the II Council of Seville (619) and the IV of Toledo (633).

In homage to the two bishops, Seville included them in the city's coat of arms. They can be seen seated on the episcopal seat on either side of Fernando the Saint. Their religious and intellectual work which brought the name of Seville to all Europe was thus recognized.

The rise of Seville under the Visigoths was interrupted by the Arabs from across the Straits of Gibraltar. The arrival of the sons of Witiza was to open a new era in the history of the city.

CHAPTER IV

ISBILIYA MORA

The Moslem Conquest

When reference is made to the Seville of the Moslem era, one can get the impression that the five centuries of Arab domination was one long homogeneous period –that from conquest to reconquest everything was run by a series of basically similar rulers. Nothing could be further from the truth.

The Islamic period in Seville –or Isbiliya as it was to be known from then on– was of such duration that changes of an extremely diverse nature took place. Moreover, the conquerers were of widely differing origin and had their own particular backround and training in Islam. Successive waves of Yemenites, Syrians, Berbers, Asians and North Africans reached Seville, though never in such profusion as to outnumber the native Hispanic-Visigoth population.

Though there were some notable instances of fusion of the cultures, the Moslem conquerers, in effect, superimposed themselves on a native population that continued to practice its religion, customs and language. While the Islamic presence left an important mark on Seville, it would be a mistake to believe that the real historical essence of what the city was to become in the future was created in these centuries.

When did the Islamic invaders first arrive in our city? On Witiza's death in the year 710, his three sons, unhappy that Rodrigo had been chosen to succeed him, called on Count Don Julian, governor of Ceuta, to raise the Islamic troops in North Africa. The following year their army landed in Gibraltar and defeated Rodrigo's soldiers at the battle of Guadalete.

The invaders were to wait a year before seizing Seville. The city was initially taken without resistance by the Moor Muza; those Sevillians opposed to the new ruler escaping to Niebla and Beja. Muza's troops were not numerous, however, and in order to consolidate the conquest he had to entrust the Jewish population with the defence of the city. The Christians who had chosen to remain in the city called on their departed brethren for assitance in organizing a rebellion. Muza's son, Abd-el-Aziz was forced to return to occupy the city by force.

From this moment on, Jews, Arabs and Christians would make up the population of Seville, until Christian troops under Fernando the Third (The Saint) reconquered the city half a milenium later.

The most important groups of invaders were the *Adnanies* and the *Yemenites* together with a few *Berbers* from North Africa. Whilst their overall numbers were not to exceed 18,000, they were soon joined by the *Muladies*, Spanish-Visigoths who opted to embrace the Moslem faith. This group was comprised of the most important families in Seville; families like the Banu Sabarico or the Banu Jaldun. The Islamization of these aristocrats did not signify pacific submission to the conquerers, however. They organized a series of revolts to retain the power and the privileges they had enjoyed up until then, both in the city and on their huge estates.

Seville was entering a period of turbulence where old and new nobles struggled for power, and tribal revolts were stirred up by those from across the Strait.

From Emirate to Caliphate

The first stage in the Arab conquest of Seville would see Al-Andalus –the Islamized part of the Iberian peninsula– become an emirate under the rule of the Caliph of Damascus, a member of the Omeya family.

Abd-el-Aziz was appointed Emir of these lands and Isbiliya became his capital. He fell in love with the Christian Egilona, widow of Rodrigo, the last Visigoth King. It would seem that cohabitation with this lady led him to change his thinking somewhat, to the extent of becoming overly influenced by indigenous ways. Legend has it that this was the reason for his assassination at the hands of fellow Moslems not content with his change of mind. All evidence points to his death as the cause of the frequent tribal wars which flared up during the first stage of the conquest.

In the middle of the eighth century, the Omeya family were replaced by the Abbasies as rulers of the Caliphate and the capital moved from Damascus to Baghdad. Abderraman I, an Omeya forced to flee by this change of circumstance, landed in Almunecar, and managed to get himself proclaimed Emir. He moved the capital to Cordoba in the year 756.

Seville, none too happy with the transfer of capital status to a neighbouring city, battled to achieve greater autonomy with respect to Cordoba. Seville had to content itself with being capital of one of the *coras*, or provinces, into which Al-Andalus, for administrative purposes, had been divided. A *wali* or governor was in overall control, assisted by a *caid*, commander of the armed forces.

These were dark and difficult years for the people of Seville; years of social unrest, hunger and epidemics that swept through the south of the Peninsula.

To these calamities was to be added the Norman invasion in the late ninth century when Abderraman II was Emir. The *Machus*, as the Arabs called them, attacked Lisbon before moving on to Sanlucar, from there to sail up the river Guadalquiver and strike at Coria del Rio. They reached Sevilla on the Ist of October, 844 and proceeded to sack and pillage, destroy and murder for three whole days. From Cordoba the Emirate sent an army out to meet them and the two armies crossed swords near Tablada. Though the outcome of the battle is far from clear, the Normans were able to continue their violent journey along the banks of the Guadalquiver for at least another month.

Isbiliya lived through difficult times as a result of the new invasion, but the Norman aggression did have its positive side. With the aim of avoiding further attacks of this nature, Abderraman II ordered the rebuilding of the city walls –then in a pitiable state. The city's boundaries were redrawn to cater for the influx of numerous families seeking refuge in the metropolis.

Conscious of the need for a powerful navy to patrol the coasts for enemy ships, the Emir called for the construction of dockyards for shipbuilding. Their exact location is not known but must have been in the Arenal area.

During Abderraman II's reign and prior to the Norman invasion the first great mosque was built in Isbiliya, and over the course of the Arab conquest several more were to be built. The mosque served as the religious centre of the city whilst the "zoco" or market became its economic centre. The Great Mosque was situated in what had always been the centre of the city: on the site occupied today by the El Salvador church.

A part of the half-buried patio or courtyard is one of the few archeological relics of the Emirate. Its structure, severely damaged during the Norman invasion, was further debilitated by an earthquake in 1079. The mosque had eleven naves, fifty metres in width and a little less in length.

In spite of the calamities suffered by Seville in these years, the period of Abderraman II was one of the most fruitful for the city. The years following the Viking invasion were years of peace and stability and tolerance between the various ethnic groups. The Mozarabic population, in other words the Christian community, continued to be numerous, and were represented before the Islamic authorities by their archbishop, given that Sevilla continued to be metropolitan –in the religious sense.

Recafredo, the most prominent archbishop of this epoch, presided over the Council of Cordoba in 852, called for the purpose of ending the violent confrontations between sections of the Christian and Moslem populations.

The generally peaceful coexistence which followed came to an end during the last decade of the ninth century, when the Arabs and Muladies sought to break away from Cordoban control. The Sevillians were loathe to accept the supremacy of their neighbours. Cordoban power was, however, sufficient not only to quell the rebellion but, in fact, to consolidate itself with the proclamation of Abderraman III as independent Caliph in the year 929.

With Cordoba now a Caliphate, Isbiliya was to witness the temporary disappearance of the spirit of rebelliousness and insubordination that had characterized the city since the first days of the conquest. The explanation for this no doubt lies with the strengthening of central power, effectively undermining the influence of Seville's wayward families. To preempt further outbreaks of rebellion, Abderraman III ordered the destruction of the city walls.

Cordoba's protagonism was such that Seville found itself overshadowed with respect to Al-Andalus. Still, the climate of peace favoured a certain cultural upsurge in the city, if only as a reflection of the splendour of the Caliphate Court. The fame of distinguished Andalusian authors, artists and teachers of this period spread far beyond the frontiers of Islamized Spain. However, the chronicles which have come down to us from those times are not very explicit in so far as our city is concerned. Perhaps the saying "no news is good news" is applicable in the historical sense as well.

Already in Almanzor's days the Cordoban Caliphate had begun its decline, and disintegratory tendancies were once more to assert themselves in the face of this debilitation.

Seville, Taifa Kingdom

Very soon Al-Andalus changed from Caliphate to Taifa Kingdoms. For Isbilaya the opportunity had arrived to seize power from its rival, Cordoba. When the Cordoban Caliphate finally fell, Seville became an independant territory with the *cadi* Ibn Abad acting as sovereign.

The establishment of Seville as a Taifa kingdom called for at least, a semblance of legality. This gave rise to the most picturesque episode in the history of Islamic Seville: the creation of a fake Caliph. A Sevillian artisan bearing a physical resemblance to the Caliph Hixam II, who was believed to have died in strange circumstances, was induced to impersonate him. Fiction was accepted as reality and a considerable number of families accepted his sovereignty.

However, the kingdom of Seville was only really consolidated under Almutadid, the son of Ibn-Abbad. Still supposedly acting under the orders of the fake Caliph, he extended the frontiers of the Seville Kingdom to take in Carmona, Badajoz, Niebla and Huelva. He lured the chiefs of other areas, men like Arcos, Moron and Ronda to Seville, and once there, manoevred them adroitly into one of the baths which he then had walled over. Algeciras was later added to the new independant kingdom.

In this way Seville soon became the most important Taifa kingdom in Al-Andalus. Almutadid, in spite of his apparent power, was forced to pay tribute to the Christian Kings who were advancing steadily towards the South and pressurizing the Taifa kingdoms. In 1063, Fernando I of Castille attacked the Kingdom of Seville and Almutadid was forced to pay the corresponding homages. The Christian King requested the transfer of the body of Saint Isidor to be moved to Leon.

Almutadid was succeeded by his son Almutamid, who was born in 1039 in the city of Beja and educated in his father's court. His love of poetry and love and war earned him the name "Poet King". During his reign, Seville advanced considerably in the political and cultural fields. His dominion extended from the Algarve in the West to Murcia in the east. Isbiliya attracted artists and literary figures from afar, drawn by the generosity and patronage of its famous King.

The "Alcazar", the King's palace, the nucleus of which today still stands, became the centre for literary soirées. In the many buildings of Al-Mubarak (The Blessed)'s palace or in the heavily scented gardens there were poetry readings, musical recitals, and wine flowing in abundance. The rigid precepts of Islamic religion were relaxed and the refinement of courtly life contrasted with the coarseness of the days of the conquest.

Although this palace is the only one to have survived intact, there were others in the Seville of Almutamid. His personal preference was for a smaller one with a beautiful view looking out over the Guadalquivir.

Seville was an important centre for music. Musical instruments were made here and musicians from the city were renowned throughout Al-Andalus. It was even said that when a musician died in Cordoba, his instruments had to be brought to Seville to find a buyer.

The cultured and refined atmosphere of the city had an effect on clothing habits and personal hygiene. The numerous bathing houses had both hygienic and religious uses. The people wore turbans (not a widespread custom in the rest of Al-Andalus) and let one of its ends fall over the shoulders. The men dressed in full-length wide-sleeved tunics worn over their trousers. The women covered their faces with a veil or with a tunic which covered them from head to toe. This tradition seems to have been relaxed in Seville under the influence of Jewish and Christian traditions where the face was allowed to be uncovered.

The Seville elite were refined in as far as food was concerned. Arab recipes from those times illustrate the richness of the cuisine. Pantries would include a wide variety of items such as dried figs, raisins and almonds, and literary works make reference to sofisticated gastronomic habits. Almutamid was especially fond of a dish of stewed rabbit and snails. Just as the three religions in Seville were tolerated, so were the three different ways of preparing food: the Andalusian, the Christian and the Jewish.

Almutamid's immersion in courtly affairs was to have fatal repercussions for the unity of his kingdom, the frontiers of which were under renewed attack from Christian Kings. Alfonso VI of Castille asked for more homages, and when these were not paid he laid siege to Seville for three days. Unable to confront the situation with his own forces, the Taifa King was forced to seek help from the Almoravids from across the Strait.

The Almoravids were a Berber people from the Maghreb area whose severity and religious puritanism had quickly extended over the entire face of North Africa. Their philosophy was a long way from that of the Poet King, but under such pressure from the Christians, they were his only possibility. Though the request was a success in terms of achieving the general objective, it was to prove ominous for Almutamid himself, who was exiled from his beloved Seville by the new invaders. The Almoravids crossed the Strait and defeated the Castillian troops at the battle of Zalaca (1086).

The Almoravid presence in the Peninsula breathed new life into the exhausted Islamic forces, divided and weakened by the Taifa phenomenon. The Almoravids, who had themselves set their sights on these lands, took advantage of the incessant bickering between the kingdoms to usurp them of their powers.

Seville fell to the Almoravids in 1091. Almutamid, now in exile, wandered through Tangiers and Meknes before dying in Agmat several years later.

Though little is known about the 56 year residence of the Almoravids in Seville, their presence does not appear to have been either significant or important for the city. We do know, however, that it was used as a base for further conquests and that, to the relief of the inhabitants, many of the burdensome taxes were lifted.

The contrast between these rugged desert warriors and the refined and cultured Seville of Almutamid must surely have been dramatic. The laxity pertaining to religious practices was replaced by strictness to the requirements of the Koran, and religious tolerance was followed by severity of treatment for those not following the doctrine of Mohammed. However, the Almoravids were attracted to the life style of the people of Seville and, as the years went by, began to live in greater harmony with them.

In other respects the Almoravid conquest can have affected the daily life of Sevillians only in as much as it offered the people greater peace of mind in the face of the Christian threat.

Seville under the Almohades

A new invasion from North Africa was to force Seville to take a new turn. This time it was to be the Almohades, and their presence in the city would leave a deeper mark than any of their predecessors and contribute to it reaching a position not attained since the Moslem conquest.

The Almohades, originally from the Moroccan Atlas area, were more universalist than the Almoravides. They began expanding around the third decade of the twelfth century and crossed the Strait in 1146. A year later they took control of Seville and lost no time in choosing it as the capital of Al-Andalus.

From this moment onward, Islamic Seville went from strength to strength until reaching its zenith between 1163 and 1184, during the reign of the Abu Yacub Yusuf.

The rapid conquest of Andalusia by the Almohades brought peace to the region and encouraged a series of very positive developments for the city. What remains today of Islamic Seville is largely from this period.

The city's perimeter was enlarged and exactly defined by the reconstruction of the city walls, which were to stay intact until well into the nineteenth century. Some of the wall faces in the Macarena area can still be seen and bear testimony to the simplicity and solidity of their construction. They were built not only for protection against outside enemies but also against the flooding of the river.

There were twelve gates and two postern gates, their names alluding to the access they allowed to respective suburbs or cities (Osario, Macarena, Carmona etc.).

The bridge over the Guadalquivir facilitated communication with the opposite bank of the river and the Aljarife area. It was a bridge resting on barges fastened together by a hefty iron chain, anchored at both ends by solid pillars sunk into the riverbed.

As in other times the Guadalquivir –meaning "great river" in Arabic– constituted a vital artery for the city along which flowed a large part of its riches. Everything from olive oil and wheat to building materials was continuously being loaded or unloaded on oar or sail-powered ships, adding a dash of colour and life to the landscape.

From the banks of the Guadalquiver rose the splendid Torre del Oro (Tower of Gold), built by Abn-Al-Ula in 1221. By being able to control navegation on the river it formed another link in the city's defence. When the chain connected to the other bank was tensed, no ship could pass beyond that point. The exterior of the tower was covered in glazed tiles, the colour of which gave it its name.

A new palace was also built in this period on allotments outside the city in a place known as Al-Buhayra. Luxuriant gardens were designed next to the building and a wall constructed around the palace and grounds.

The fact that people could receive drinking water in their houses thanks to the construction of a large irrigation channel, proves the level of advancement attained by Isbiliya during these years.

Of all the works of the Almohade epoch, none can compare with the Great Mosque with its famous minaret –later to be christened La Giralda.

The old mosque, built three centuries earlier, could not house all the Moslems in this very religious city whose population had grown and attained a high level of development. The architect Ben-Baso was commissioned for the design of the new mosque. Unfortunately, the monument has not survived in its entirety as the cathedral was later built over it. We do know, however, that it was roughly the same size as the Cordoban mosque. It had a dome over the *mihrab*, a wooden ceiling and was decorated with fine materials –ebony, sandalwood, gold and marble.

The most admired part of the mosque was the minaret. Very high and solidly built, it was also extraordinarily elegant and beautiful. Its perfection can only be compared to the Kutubia in Marrackesh or the Hassan tower in Rabat, with which it bears a certain relation stylistically. But, without doubt, it was more spectacular than both.

The tower took longer to finish than the rest of the mosque. To commemorate the defeat of Alfonso VIII at the battle of Alarcos, it was decided to place four globes of decreasing diameter, finished in thick laminas of gold, in the upper part of the tower. The completed work must have looked very different to what is visible today due to alterations carried out in the eighteenth century.

Seville can be grateful to the impetus of Abu Yacub Yusuf for important urban and monumental changes. It is still fascinating

44

to think that an instransigent and nomadic people like the Almohades were capable of carrying out works of such creative calibre in the city they elected capital. However, we should not forget the ability of Seville to exercise a peculiar charm over those who came to settle here, wherever they were from.

The construction fever and splendour of this period was cut short by the Christian advance. The battle of Alarcos was to have its reply in the battle of las Navas de Toloso in 1212, and signal the beginning of Almohade decadency. Again, as the Caliph's powers diminished, confrontations and divisions between the different factions in Seville reappeared, facilitating the Christian reconquest.

In 1245 Isbiliya signed an accord with Fernando III, in which his authority was recognized as well as the obligation of paying taxes. The ensuing revolts and protests against the accord served as the pretext for the military intervention of the Rey Santo (Saint King).

At the end of November of 1248 Seville was reconquered by the Castille Crown.

CHAPTER V

THE SAINT KING AND THE WISE KING

The Reconquest

After the Reconquest of Seville a historical treatment must inevitably be less narrative than it has been up to now. On the one hand less events occur –in the sense of things happening that completely alter the trajectory of the city. On the other hand, historians have much more data available than the simple chronicles of contemporaries. From this point on the increase in the amount of information available allows us to reach a deeper understanding of history– something impossible in the more distant past. Demography, economics and the organization of social and administrative affairs are some of the areas about which we have increasing data as we reach the present day.

When Fernando III decided to conquer Seville, he was fully aware that the city walls were impregnable with the means he had at his disposal. He had no option but to lay siege to it and hope that the inhabitants would be forced by hunger to surrender.

The Christian King considered Seville to be of vital importance to the Spanish Almohades, and strategically placed with regard to the South of the Peninsula.

Once Jaen had been conquered, Fernando moved on to take control of Carmona, Lora, Cantillana and Alcala del Rio. He was then able to place an army commanded by Pelay Correa in the outskirts of Seville. The siege was, however, to last two years, during which time whole forests were cut down and several other outlying towns recaptured. The decisive blow was struck with the aid of Admiral Bonifaz, who sailed up the Guadalquivir with his fleet and destroyed the bridge linking Seville with the Triana area, thus cutting off supply lines from the Aljarife zone. Hunger was to deliver the city into the hands of Fernando III who entered the capital of Al-Andalus on St Clements Day, 22 December, 1248.

Fernando, canonized by the Catholic Church in the eighteenth century, was born in Zamora in the year 1201, and when both Leon and Castille came under the same Crown, he decided the time was ripe for the Reconquest. His work for the unification of Spain was decisive. He also protected both the Church and culture. His association with Seville was such that he made his home there until shortly before his death, in 1252. Seville recognized his patronage by including him in the city's coat of arms. The historian Morgado described the coat of arms as showing "...the Saint King Don Fernando seated in his Court, a naked sword held high in his right hand and a globe in his left, flanked by the glorious brothers Leandro and Isidore, patrons of Seville and his prelates".

After the fall of Seville to the Christians, many other towns and villages surrendered without resistance. Soon the whole of the Guadalquivir valley was in their hands.

As Alfonso X the Wise recounts, once the city had been conquered, King Fernando gave the Moors one month to sell what possessions they could not bring with them and leave the city. When this time had elapsed, five ships and eight galleys were put at the disposal of those wishing to travel by sea. Those preferring to journey overland were provided with two beasts of burden and army protection to the border with Moslem Spain.

After the conquest, Seville was almost entirely without a Moslem population. Only a few groups of any size remained in neighbouring areas under agreement with the Saint King. The Moors living under Christian dominion were given the name *Mudejares*.

Alfonso X, on succeeding his father, continued to expand the frontiers of Christian Spain, conquering the cities Niebla, Ecija,

Moron, Cadiz, Medina Sidonia and Arcos. He ordered the rehabilitation of the Seville dockyards for the purpose of building ships for an expedition to North Africa. Remains of the dockyard at the Santa Caridad hospital give some idea of its magnitude.

Alfonso X, unlike his father, considered the Mudejares settled near the frontier to be a potential danger. He thus decided to eject them and close off access to the sea of the entire area around the river Guadalete, all of which culminated in the Mudejar revolt of 1262.

The Moors of Jerez, Arcos, Lebrija, Utrera and other cities joined forces against Alfonso X, and it would seem that one of their plans was nothing less than to kidnap the Royal Family in Seville and occupy the city. The plot was discovered and the attempt ended in failure. It did, nevertheless, succeed in other areas; in Arcos, Vejer, Rota and Sanlucar de Barrameda. Alfonso X's response was rapid and severe. Once the rebellion had been crushed, he ordered the repatriation of all Mudejeres in the Kingdom of Granada to the North of Africa.

It was at this stage that the Moslem population disappeared from Spain. All that remained of their five century stay were the monuments that still stood intact and the memory of an era where people of such distinct character and origin contributed to make the city more open and cosmopolitan.

Alfonso X felt the same attraction to Seville as his father had done. Born in Toledo in 1221, he inherited the right to be named Emperor of the Sacred Romano-German Empire through his marriage to Beatrice of Swabia –though opposition from the Papacy prevented him from ever taking up the title. His work in cultural areas was impressive. He encouraged the development of the Castillian language, renovated the Toledan School of Translators, systematized and unified the Law in his dominions, and encouraged the study of astronomy. His work represented the cultural fusion of the West and the Orient and the three religious communities within his Kingdom: the Christian, the Jewish and the Moslem.

Although his work in these area proved to be highly positive, earning him the name of Alfonso the Wise, as a politician he left a lot to be desired. His clumsiness alienated him from his subjects, and he created the enmity of his son and heir Don Sancho on making some concessions to the "Infantes de la Cerda", the sons of his first-born son Fernando de la Cerda, who had died prematurely.

In his confrontation with his son, Alfonso the Wise felt abandoned by all and sunder, and only the city of Seville remained loyal to him. For this reason he was to add his oft recited epithet, "NO MADEXADO", to his coat of arms.

When he died in 1284, he was buried alongside his father in the Santa Maria Church, and both tombs can presently be viewed in the Royal Chapel in Seville Cathedral.

The Repopulation

One of the most pressing problems for the Christian kings of the reconquest was the repopulation of areas left vacant by the Moors, to guard against their possible repossession.

In a sparsely populated country, as Spain was at that time, it was no easy matter persuading people to move to frontier regions where the danger of attacks and *razzias* from the Moors was a very real one. To encourage repopulation, the kings had to offer incentives and privileges to those willing to run these risks.

We are fortunate in having detailed information about the repopulation of these areas thanks to the *libros de repartimiento* (books of redistribution), which include reports from the people who settled there. The redistribution was carried out in two different ways. There was the *donadío*, property donated by the King as reward for the nobles, institutions and clergy who had contributed to the reconquest and which involved military obligations to the Crown. Some of the properties were extensive, to say the least, and formed the basis of the power and wealth of their beneficiaries.

The other form of distribution was called *heredamiento* or endowment. This was land reserved for the city council to divide out amongst the people. To receive land the beneficiary had to have his main house in the city, abide by the laws, and was prohibited to sell the land within a period of five years. The size of these estates was much smaller than the "donadios".

The lecturer Julio Gonzalez produced an excellent report of the distribution of Seville. He gives details of how both Fernando III and his son Alfonso X took into account those who had contributed to the campaign and the interests of the Crown when the time came to divide out the land.

To counterbalance the power and influence of the nobles, the Kings kept Seville under their own personal jurisdiction. Those who received land, whether donated by the King or by the City Council, were bound by a series of obligations linked to the defense of the territory.

Responsibility for the redistribution of Seville fell to the "Junta de partidores" (Distribution board), which was, in effect, the Town Council.

The new map would show numerous small and middle-sized landowners and a small group of landed gentry with extensive properties. The latter were fortunate to receive the majority of their land in the rich Aljarife region. In time they were to go increasing their power and wealth until they more or less controlled the city administration.

The beneficiaries of the share-out came, in the main part, from Castille, though Leon, Asturias, Galicia and Catalonia were also represented.

The Control of Municipal Power

The Benimerines of North Africa crossed the Strait at the end of the thirteenth century and began to attack Christian positions. Their efforts were not sufficient to make an impact on what was then happening in the Peninsula. The advance of the Castillian-Leonian Kings was now unstoppable and both Sancho IV and his successor Fernando IV pushed the frontier southwards.

During these years the great families of the nobility began to struggle amongst themselves for municipal control of Seville.

Since the days of the reconquest the city of Seville was governed by a town-council, made up of a representative section of the population. Members of the lower nobility –the *gentry*– sat alongside delegates of the *common* people. The gentry were also called the *venticuatros* (twenty four), their original number, though this was to increase notably in later years.

The Council was also responsible for the administration of justice, through its first three, then later four *alcaldes mayores* (lord mayors). They were appointed by the King and presided over the municipal council.

Seville council's jurisdiction extended beyond the boundaries of the city over a wide rural area –the so-called *alfoz* or area surrounding Seville. Alfonso X gave this name to the three different regions making up Seville: el Aljarafe, whose agricultural wealth was based on the numerous olive groves; la Ribera, a marshy zone dedicated to livestock farming; and lastly, la Campiña, a cereal growing region with scattered though populous townships.

Ramon Carande, in a study of early medieval Seville, pointed out the importance of the Alfoz as food supplier to the city. The production methods and transport systems of that time would have posed serious problems for the supply of essentials from further afield.

Fernando IV, in granting the Seville council control of fiscal matters, gave it the power to impose and collect taxes within the area under its jurisdiction. The possibilities that such power entailed unleashed the ambitions of the nobility, especially the Guzmán, Ponce de León and La Cerda families. This oligarchy struggled continuously throughout the fourteenth and fifteenth centuries for exclusive governmental control of Seville.

Alfonso XI (1325-1350) issued a series of decrees placing the government of the city in the hands of the gentry. It was an attempt to reinforce the position of the lesser nobility in the face of the powerful aristocratic families' ambitions, and thus reaffirm Royal control.

His successor, Pedro I (1350-1369), took the same line of approach, but his despotism and cruelty led to abuses, many of which arose from internal strife within the Royal Family itself.

He ordered the executions of Alonso Fernandez Coronel, Juan de La Cerda, his stepbrother Don Fadrique and the Queen herself, Blanca de Borbon, accused of adultery. The war against his bastard brother Enrique de Trastamara, son of Alfonso XI and his Sevillian concubine Leonor de Guzman, resulted in more executions and earned him the name "The Cruel."

Enrique de Trastamara's definitive victory spelled the end of Pedro I's authoritarian regime and the granting of greater powers to the nobility, who managed to squeeze more titles and privileges out of the new King. His successor Juan I (1379-1390) was unable to stop the consolidation of the power of the nobility, nor their gradual takeover of the Sevillian Local Authority. They had succeeded in tying their interests to members of the gentry who held decision-making positions in the city administration. In the years that followed a struggle developed between the houses of Guzman and Ponce de Leon for control of the city. In the ensuing confusion an attempt was made, in 1433, to follow the lead of the Italian states of the time and declare Seville an Independant Republic. The attempt failed and remains a simple anecdote in the turbulent political history of Seville in that period.

During his reign, Enrique III, with more authority than his predecessor, created the position of *corregidor* to represent the Crown and put an end to the nobility's power struggles for control of Seville. His initiative, however, was not taken up by his successor Juan II, who once again reinforced the power of the nobles. The Guzman family were given a dukedom in 1445 and the Ponce de Leons made Counts of Arcos in 1440. Both houses consolidated their control over the Seville Municipal Council and, for a short time, even managed to reach an agreement, so as to avoid any interference which might affect their interests.

On the death of Enrique IV, both his daughter Juana and his sister Isabel (the future Isabel the Catholic) claimed their right to the throne. A dispute arose between those in favour of granting more powers to the nobility –who backed the former– and those who preferred the authority of the Crown, who were backing Isabel.

The Guzmans, together with three important Castillian houses, supported Isabel. Though their stance may sound contradictory, their reasoning was that a strong monarchy would inevitably need the support of the nobles, and their interests would not therefore be put in jeopardy. The Ponce de Leon house, on the other hand, backed the Marquess of Villena, with whom they were related by marriage, and who had become Juana la Beltraneja's principal defender. Fighting between the two factions of the nobility flared up in Seville. The task of pacification of the nobles was to fall to the new Queen, Isabel of Castille, who involved them in the formidable task of the construction of a new State.

Late Medieval Seville

Alfonso the Wise eulogized Seville in the *Primera Crónica General de España* (First General Chronicle of Spain) when he wrote, "A town so well situated and simple exists nowhere else in the world...How could a city so finished and perfect and where there is such abundance and plenty be anything else but great and esteemed?"

Seville, in spite of such significant changes in the mid-thirteenth century, continued to hold a splendid strategic position with regard to communications and commerce in the south west of the peninsula. With such growth potential its gradual economic and demographic growth (not without some ups and downs, however) over the following years should not surprise us.

Fernando III had left Seville without a population. Into its deserted streets poured hords of people from the north bringing the number of inhabitants to some 24,000 in total. With the flight of rebels involved in the the Mudejar uprising of 1264 numbers dropped however, and the fourteenth century was to bring plagues and epidemics in its wake reducing the population to around 15,000. Fortunately, a significant demographic upturn at the end of the Middle Ages increased the number of inhabitants to 40,000.

The economic base of the Seville elite lay in land ownership.

This elite had its origins in the two hundred nobles who had benefited from the re-allocation of land, plus those who had were adding to their ranks for their services to the Crown. The size of individual fortunes varied in proportion to the acreage and richness of lands under their possession. From Enrique II's reign onwards the aristocracy began to suffer the effects of inbreeding and from the establishment of *primogeniture*-in which the entire family wealth was inherited by the first-born son. In the fifteenth century one of the richest houses, the Ducal de Medina Sidonia, accrued rents of four times the value of the city's municipal revenues. This gives some idea of the power of a nobility ever eager to control the mechanisms of local politics.

In urban Seville the predominant group demographically were the artisans. Whilst their economy was based on the manufacture of products, the other group, the peasantry, were responsible for catering for the city's agricultural needs. Both groups met at the weekly markets held in different parts of the city, and at the annual fair where traders travelled from far and wide to bring products not normally available in Seville.

Guilds of Artisans working in the same commercial sector were slow to form in Seville, but in the textile, leather and metalwork sectors there did exist important associations of artisans.

In this period Seville expanded as a financial and commercial centre, the control of which was in the hands of both Jews and foreigners.

When Seville returned to Christian control there were no Jews amongst its population. Soon they arrived from far and near, even from the Kingdom of Granada. The Christian Kings protected their religious practices and benefited from their business and financial expertise. The city's Jewish population was to reach a peak of two thousand in the fifteenth century. The Jews worked as money-lenders, collectors of Royal taxes, bankers etc., and in specific professions such as doctors, weavers and silversmiths.

Seville's Jewish community was located in what are today the barrios of Santa Cruz, Santa Maria la Blanca and San Bartolome. In 1391, the Christians turned on the Jews, the collectors of

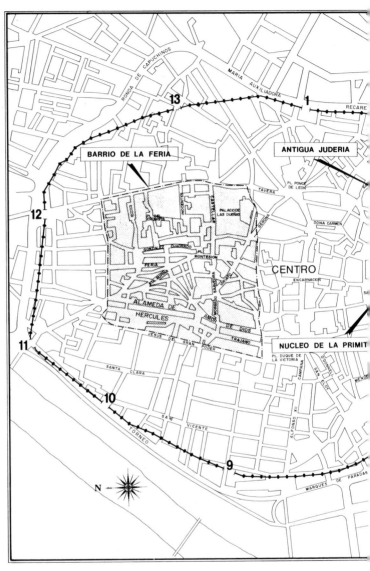

Map of Seville showing the gates of the city walls, and the most historically significant places from the Medieval period to the crisis of the XVII century.

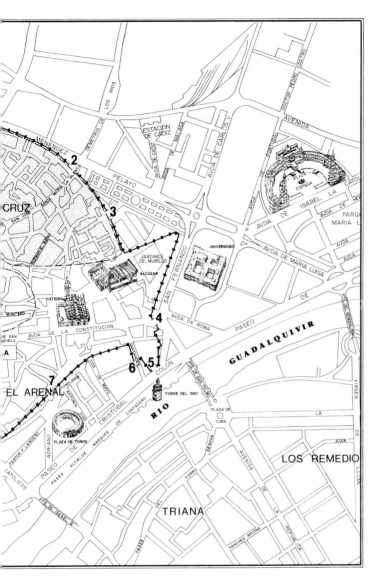

Gates:
1. Osario
2. Carmona
3. Minjoar
4. Jerez
5. Carbón
6. Aceite
7. Arenal
8. Triana
9. Goles
10. Ingenio
11. Bibarragel
12. Macarena
13. Córdoba

57

taxes and managers of money, at a time when the city was in economic crisis. Though the incident was not to have precedents, there was considerable violence and plundering. To escape persecution many Jews fled the city while others chose to remain and embrace the Christian faith. The Jewish population was, as a consequence, reduced to only seventy families.

Commercial activities in Seville were largely in the hands of foreigners who settled in the city attracted by the its position as centre of a region which imported and exported products from as far away as the North of Europe, Italy and the Mahgreb.

The fact that the foreigner's district within the city was called the *Barrio de Francos* (district of exemptions) is evidence of the tax exemptions and privileges they enjoyed. It was situated in the area surrounding the street which now bears its name.

Though there were communities of Breton, Gascon and Flemish people in Seville, by far the most important was the Genoese community, who made their living exporting agricultural produce such as cooking oil, cereals and wine from the region. Many of them settled here and names like Spinola, Centurion and Salvago have been passed down from generation to generation so many times that they have become accepted as Sevillian names.

After the reconquest, the Seville Church was headed by Archbishop Don Remondo, who succeeded in raising it to the same status as that the Toledan one, the most important in Castille. The majority of the considerable income raised from *diezmos* (tithes) and from land donated by the crown was divided up between the less than a thousand clergymen.

Apart from the secular clergy, there were more than thirty communities of regular clergy –Dominicans, Fransiscans, Carmelites, Agustinians were amongst those represented. The Cistercian San Isidorp del Campo monastery, built in Santiponce in the early fifteenth century, was one of the most important. The San Clemente and Santa Clara convents were examples of thirteenth century convents.

Although Seville had taken on a more cosmopolitan and European air since the Christian conquest, architecturally it continued to have an unmistakably Moorish look. Some of the the narrow and winding streets were cul-de-sacs *(adarves)* which ended in a small square. The houses were, on the whole, modest affairs constructed of brick, roof tiles and plaster, all painted with lime. Normally they did not exceed two floors and the few openings for windows looked out on a central patio. The fifteenth century saw new urbanistic developments in the barrios of San Lorenzo and San Vicente and in the Omnium Sanctorum area.

After Fernando III's troops had entered Seville, the old mosques were gradually transformed into Christian temples. The fusion of Christian and Islamic artistic elements gave rise to the "mudejar" phenomenon, a strong influence on the architecture of temples and civic buildings of the period. The Alcazar of the Islamic era was enlarged and reconstructed by master builders from Granada, combining both Christian and Moorish styles.

It was the Gothic style, however, that would inspire the most magnificent construction of Christian Seville. Work began on the cathedral on the site of the old Almohade mosque in 1402. It was to become one of the greatest temples of the Christian world. Its five huge naves, its main retable, its choir and its porticos make this temple the greatest architectural gem to be bequeathed to the city by history.

CHAPTER VI

THE SEVILLE OF THE AUSTRIAS

Seville and the Discovery of America

The discovery of America changed the destiny of Seville. The city which had prior to 1492 played a key role in relations between the Peninsula and the Northern part of Africa, and which for centuries had played host to the most advanced cultures of the Western Mediterranean, was now to turn its gaze westward to capitalize on its privileged position on the route to the New World.

This historic event, which took place during the reign of Isabel I of Castille and Fernando II of Aragon, the so-called "Reyes Catolicas" (Catholic Kings), was to close the curtain on the Medieval period and open up a new historical era that would bring Seville its moments of greatest splendour.

The discovery fever had already begun during the last stages of the Middle Ages. Western man's need for a range of commodities considered vital for the maintenance of a life style to which he had grown accustomed, led him to open up new routes to obtain them. Spices from the Orient, silk from China, cotton from India or precious stones from Southern Africa, were sufficient impetus for traders to undertake long voyages in search of what was sure to be good business.

Whilst these products were much sought after in Europe, it was gold, now a necessity for mercantile activity for its exchange value, whose sources were most earnestly sought.

During the last years of the Middle Ages there had been a real scarcity of the means of payment, a situation worsened by the Turkish conquest of Santos Lugares in 1453. The route normally taken by Western merchants was thus blocked, forcing them to look for a new route to reach the Orient via the western coast of Africa that would avoid the Ottoman empire.

Thanks to their geographical position and maritime experience, the Portuguese were the first to embark on the new route. Since the beginning of the fifteenth century, however, expeditions in this direction had left from the western coast of Andalusia. Sponsored by nobles such as the Duke of Medina Sidonia or the Marquess of Cadiz, for such enterprises as fishing and commerce, Andalusian sailors had begun to gain experience in Atlantic navegation. The conquest of the Canary islands, was to be one of the fruits of such missions. For John Elliot, the great British scholar of Spain, "The occupation of the Canaries by Castille was an event of great importance in maritime history. Their geographical situation would make them an indispensible step in the route to America. Columbus' four expeditions took on supplies in the Canary Archipelago. At the same time they served as a perfect laboratory for Castillian colonial experiments and formed a natural link between the Spanish Reconquest and the Conquest of America."

All these expeditions left from Ayamonte or Cadiz, a part of the Andalusian coast that had formely been the territory of the Kingdom of Seville. It was no accident that these ports were chosen. They were ideally placed in relation to the trade winds so vital in those days of sailing ships, to the extent that any ship travelling west was obliged to take this route.

The Castillian Kings, in an effort to stop any interference in relations being established with the New World, decided on a system of protection wherein ships bound for or returning from America could dock in only one port. That privilege was to go to Seville.

Why was Seville chosen and not one of seaside ports with a geographical position seemingly more suitable for guarding exclusivity with the New World? The Huelvan ports were less reliable and the vast majority of the land was owned by the nobles, which would make control of maritime traffic more difficult for the Crown. On the Cadiz coast, Sanlucar de Barrameda had no sheltered harbour and Cadiz itself, though fulfilling the requirements of a monopoly port –as would be demonstrated in the eighteenth century– was at that time only a small city, isolated from the interior, and an easy target for sea raiders tempted by the riches held within its walls.

Seville was not without its disadvantages however. The Guadalquivir presented navigational problems not the least of which were the perilous sandbanks of Sanlucar. The advantages would more than compensate, however. Being an interior and well fortified port it was well placed to resist attacks from abroad. Moreover, at a distance of 84 kilometres from the sea, the control of vessels could more efficiently be carried out. Though the authorities overseeing trade with the Indies could not completely stamp out contraband, it was not the constant headache it might have been had the elected port been situated next to the sea.

The port of Seville had, before the fifteenth century, always been busy exporting the products of its fertile valleys. It was after the Discovery, however, that it became a world port and point of departure from the Old to the New Continent, and one of most important metropolis in the world.

Seville, its port and its river. For two hundred years what the distinguished French historian Pierre Chaunu called "Seville's Atlantic" was to the dominating factor in the city. The complex and varied New World was to receive the influence, control and patronage of the great Andalusian metropolis.

America was as significant for Seville as Seville was for it. Though it is certain that the rise of Seville's was very much linked to the events which ocurred in 1492, it would be difficult to understand the course of events in those territories discovered, conquered and colonized by the Castille Crown, without taking into account Seville's contribution at each one of the stages into which the conquest is traditionally divided.

Seville between the Old and New World

How and in what way did Seville carry out its role as intermediary between the Old and New worlds? Until 1550 communications between both sides of the Atlantic were both irregular and sporadic. Until then very little was known about these lands or the huge effect they were to have on the Monarchy of the Austrias. We can thus understand how the questionable system of "Free ships" came into use. Under this system, ships would make the crossing alone, with no protection whatsoever from possible attacks by pirates or privateers from other countries. They would sail without having calculated the most favourable time for navegation.

It was the rise in the level of traffic, and above all, the need to protect the cargoes of the much coveted precious metals that led to the system of sailing in convoys. Two fleets left annualy; the first setting sail in early April bound for New Spain, the other in August with a destination of Tierra Firme. Both fleets wintered in the West Indies before joining forces in Havana in March for the crossing back to Spain.

The fleets left from and returned to the port of Seville. The city was thus the starting point for the "race to the Indies", and everywhere in the city people were talking about the newly dicovered territories.

Each year the arrival of the fleet was greeted with great enthusiasm, and not surprisingly since the whole commercial system and even the Kingdom of the Austrias owed its survival to it. The fleet brought silver and riches, compensation for merchants who had sent their products to the New World. It enabled Felipe II to finance his campaigns in the Low Countries, and Felipe IV to pay off the numerous debts of the Crown.

Seville's monopoly of the race to the Indies multiplied mercantile and financial activity in the city. During the sixteenth century it reached the height of its splendour. People from Castille and from abroad came in numbers, some to settle here and share in its riches, others to embark on a journey to the New World and there look for new opportunities. This activity was to make the Andalusian capital not only one of the most populous and important cities in Europe, but also the principal financial and commercial centre of the Old Continent.

From its summit during the reign of the first three Austrians Carlos I, Felipe II and Felipe III, Seville was to fall into stagnation and economic and demographic recession from the mid eighteenth century onwards. The crisis of the Monarchy had a direct influence on the historical destiny of the city. The historian Dominguez Ortiz has pointed out that the destiny of Seville under the Austrias was closely related to the destiny of the Monarchy itself.

Imperial Spain suffered a crisis which would result in the loss of its primacy in Europe. Its vast territories began to be divided up and traffic to the Americas, which had contributed so much to its strength, began to drop off during the early decades of the seventeenth century.

Seville was more heavily affected by the crisis than any other city in the Peninsula. To make matters worse, the terrible plague of 1649 carried off a large part of the population. In addition, Cadiz began to play a more important role in trade with the Americas and eventually succeeded in capturing the port monopoly. There were geographical and technical reasons, such .as the difficulties of navegating the Guadalquivir now that ships were of a higher tonnage, as well as practical ones –pressure was mounting from merchants keen to escape the rigid control of the Seville tax authorities.

The decline was rapid and irreversible and Seville became just another city within the Kingdom. The cosmopolitanism of the Golden Age was to give way to old fashioned provincialism, more concerned with lamenting its glorious past than building a future.

The People of Seville and their activities

The heights to which Seville had risen in the fifteenth century is clearly reflected in the spectacular population growth. Already at the turn of the century there were 60,000 inhabitants. The first few decades saw some decrease due to epidemics and

Traiana

1. Las Cuebas.	5. la Rinconada.	9. Puecta de Traiano.	13. La C
2. S. Inquisitia.	6. la Mecced.	10. S. Pablo.	14. La
3. S. Laureano.	7. Puente di Traiano.	11. S. Magdalena.	15. S. P
4. Monast. del Carmen.	8. La Aßuntio.	12. S. Buenauentura.	16. S.

Period engraving showing the Port of Seville in the days of the "Race to the Indies".

emigration to the Indies, leaving the city scantily populated and according to the ambassador Andreas Navajero, in Seville for the wedding of Emperor Carlos V in 1525, "almost in the hands of women". As of these moments the population began to rise again reaching a figure of 120,000 in 1580, after Naples the most populated city in Europe.

Immigrants from the north and centre of the country and foreigners lured by the opportunity to participate in trade with the New World, had a multiplying effect on demographic figures. If to these numbers are added real population growth (more births than deaths) this dramatic increase does not seem so surprising.

The seventeenth century provided a different panorama. The sun was now setting on Seville's days of glory and there was a clear demographic crisis. The plague of 1599-1601 signalled the beginning of the change, but the real catastrophe occured in 1649 with the outbreak of the worst plague in the history of the city. The chronicler of the period, Diego Ortiz de Zunyiga, described the tradgedy in dramatic terms: "Seville suffered a huge loss of inhabitants and next to nobody was left. A large number of dwellings lie empty, surely to become ruins in the years to come. Occupied properties have lost considerable value. Public contributions are at a very low level....The militia has been almost completely disbanded; factory and trade guilds are without craftsmen and artisans; the fields lie uncultivated and people coming from other areas to work here are paid a pittance".

The plague scythed the population down to 60,000 and paralysed activities of every kind. It was a hard blow for the city and one from which recovery would prove difficult. By the end of the sixteenth century only the shadow remained of what had once been a densely populated and vital city. What at a first glance seems to be a demographic disaster was in fact symtomatic of a more general crisis affecting the whole of Castille and which was to leave it definitively weakened.

There were the rich and the poor; those who yielded political and social power and those who were marginalised. One of the characteristics of the Seville of this era was the glaring contrast in the conditions under which its inhabitants lived.

At the top of the social pyramid were the nobles. Though numerically fewer than in other Spanish cities, there were proportionately more families in the upper nobility bracket. It was a predominantly urban aristocracy: though the basis of their wealth was in the country, they had a decided preference for sumptuous houses or palaces within the city boundaries. The majority of these residences were located in the Alameda de Hercules and the San Vicente barrios and were interspersed amongst more modest dwellings.

Few of these palaces have survived intact, and some, like the El Guzman palace, have fallen to the pickaxe in recent times. The Casa de Pilato is a good example of the magnificence of these buildings. The coffered ceilings, marble and sculptures are still evidence to the Rennaiscence refinement of their owners, the Marquesses of Tarifa.

The clergy formed another group within the Seville society of that time. Like the nobility, the law granted them a series of priveleges and exemptions. But there were great differences within this group.

The archbishop was the highest ecclesiastical power in Seville. It was he who received the lion's share of the Church's income, used for the distribution of alms and relief to the city's most destitute inhabitants. The present archbishop's palace, built in the middle of the seventeenth century, gives some idea of the wealth and status of the archbishops of Seville.

The members of the Chapter of the Cathedral formed a part of what could be called the upper clergy. They were canons and other distinguished clergymen who were also entitled to partake of Church income. As their obligations were not exactly burdensome, they had time to devote to literary activities and even to business.

The lower clergy found themselves in an entirely different position. They were formed in part by those responsible for the parishes within the city, and in part by mere beneficiaries, chaplains or lay preachers. Although theoretically they were enitled to a part of the Church *tithes*, in reality they lived from their stipends and what they received for the giving of sacraments.

Seville was divided into thirty parishes and the number of clergymen would have oscillated between fifteen hundred and two thousand.

A significant number of members of other religious orders were present in the city. There were 45 monasteries and 28 convents.

The richest order was the Saint Domingus, whose monastery San Pablo housed one hundred and fifty monks. The Santa Maria de las Cuevas monastery, belonging to the Carthusian order, was another important monastery where the tomb of Christopher Columbus rested for some time.

The vast majority of Sevillians belonged to the unprivileged classes. Though they had to pay taxes, by law they were not entitled to any exemptions. The conditions under which they lived were extremely varied. They ranged from the rich merchants who had amassed considerable fortunes from trade with the Americas to the beggars who lived off charity and the *sopa boba* (soup) dished out at the monastery. In the middle bracket were the artisans who formed the ranks of the more than fifty guilds in the city.

Social mobility was extremely limited but it was possible for a rich merchant to enter into the nobility, either by buying a letter patent of nobility or marrying into the aristocracy. A picture of Seville socially would not be complete without a mention of the marginal population. Though not a part of what might be called established society, they did add a touch of colour and vitality to the animated atmosphere so characteristic of Seville under the Austrias.

The Moriscos –Moors who had accepted Christian baptism as a means of remaining in the city– numbered about 6,000 in Seville. Although they caused no serious problems for the city they were, nevertheless, expelled in 1609, after Felipe III ordered the expulsion of all those remaining on the basis that their complete integration into Christian socity was an impossibility.

During this period Seville was not without its slaves. They were negroes or Moors in the main and were a status symbol for their masters. The treatment they received was in general acceptable. At the end of the sixteenth century there were more than

6,000, though this figure was to fall appreciably in the years to follow. Less numerous were the "gitanos" (gypsies) whose nomadic lifestyle made them statistically difficult to control.

A mention should also be made of the foreigners who, as we already noted, began to settle in the city after the reconquest in 1248. The prospect of prosperous trade with the Indies brought them flooding in. Some of them, whether Genovan, Florentine or Flemish, underwent a process of Sevillianization, settling into native families and, in some instances, into the nobility itself.

The Government of the City and its Institutions

The Seville authorities cannot have found it easy to control such a rapidly expanding city. Immigrants of differing origins and social status reached the city gates, each seeking to make a quick fortune by any means possible in this city famed for its riches.

Already, in the years before the conquest there had been difficulties, and etched on the city walls are the words: "This is a city of disorder and bad government".

The Catholic Kings were personally responsible for imparting justice when they were in Seville between 1477 and 1478, but along the course of the sixteenth century the situation had worsened considerably. Felipe II received a lot of complaints from the people of Seville about bad administration and irregularities in the functioning of its courts. The Crown was, of course, reluctant to let such a key city for the monarchy fall into disorder and took continuing measures to avoid it doing so.

Fernando and Isabel revived the figure of the "Corregidor", a dignitary appointed by the King to oversee the running of the administration. At the beginning of Charles V's reign a digest of all post conquest laws and regulations was published. The number of Lord Mayors and Aldermen as well as "Jurados" –whose job it was to close the city gates at night and open them at dawn– was increased.

All posts within the Seville council were highly sought after and in the eighteenth century the Crown, to alleviate its financial situation, introduced a system by which these posts could be bought and sold. The demand for these positions and the lucrative business their sale represented, vastly overstaffed the administration.

In 1527, work began on the construction of a building, designed by Diego de Riaño, to house all the council's off-shoots. Today, the most important departments of the Seville Council are located in this building.

Seville has the dubious honour of of being the first Spanish city to hold Inquisition trials. To resolve the problem of Jews who had been baptized Catholics but who still continued to worship the Mosaic religion, authorisation was granted by Rome for the establishment of the "Santo Oficio" or Holy Office. Headquarters were established in 1481 in the Dominican San Pablo monastery and, later, in the Castillo de Triana (Triana Castle), on the banks of the Guadalquivir.

The main task of the Holy Office was to weed out and punish false converts, and for this reason those Jews who continued to practice their faith did not see themselves affected by it. However, all Jews had to leave Seville when the Catholic Kings ordered their expulsion in 1492.

Los autos de fe, the ceremony in which sentences passed by the Inquisition were made public, took place first on the steps of the Cathedral, but was soon moved to the Plaza de San Fransisco. Huge animated crowds gathered for the whole complicated ceremony.

A political decision of great importance for the city was the founding, in 1503, of the Casa de Contratación de Indias (Indies House), to regulate and develop trade and maritime activites with the New World. Its first headquarters were in the Seville dockyards, though shortly afterwards it was moved to the Alcazar Real (Royal Palace) and installed in the Admiral's Room. In 1717 it was transferred to Cadiz.

Though it was created to force merchants to respect the interests of the Crown, as the most important cargoes were in the hands of powerful businessmen, the House soon ceased to be an instrument of official control, and, instead, came under the control of the merchants of Seville.

Trade between merchants was carried out on the steps of the cathedral, but under pressure from the council, a magnificent building was constructed between 1585 and 1598, next to the Templo Mayor, to house the Merchants market. Its architect, Juan de Herrera, had several years before directed construction of the Escorial monastery. Today, this building is the headquarters of the Archivo General de Indies (Archive of the Indies).

The University of Seville was built in the early sixteenth century. In 1502 Archdeacon Rodrigo de Santaella created its embryo, the College of Saint Mary. When permission from Rome, obligatory for its inauguration, finally arrived in 1505, teachings of the arts, logic, philosophy, theology, canon law, civil law and medicine could then commence. Classes did not start up, however, until 1516 and the number of students attending the university was far fewer than at the Salamanca or Alacala de Henares universities.

Felipe IV's court favourite, the Conde-duque de Olivares of Sevillian origin, became interested in the university and in 1623 granted it superior category, thus bringing it onto a par with universities of longer tradition. He also also granted it special legal status and put it under the guardianship of the Audiencia.

The University of Seville began life in buildings acquired by Maese Rodrigo in the Puerta de Jerez. Only the chapel, however, consecrated in 1506, now remains.

Other official institutions of that time were the High Court and the Royal prison –through whose doors passed a stream of of Seville's lumpen elements and even the odd celebrity, Miguel de Cervantes to name one.

Daily life in Seville under the Austrias

Seville passed through two very different stages during the two centuries of Austria rule; stages which Domingo Ortiz called "The rise and the decline", and which were felt in the everyday life of the city. As opposed to previous epochs no earth-shattering changes altered the day to day existence of its inhabitants. No wars, invasions from abroad or, indeed, any type of military operation disturbed the peace of its citizens.

When the Catholic Kings finally ended the War of Granada, there was no longer a justification for the leadership and military power of the nobility, something which had always been of concern to the Crown. Oligarchs and institutions were now expected to lend their services to the creation of the constitution of a new State, wherein the Crown would not be under the influence of any powerful class. Seville was faithful in this respect and did not create major problems for the monarchy. In fact it worked efficiently to construct the Empire of the Austrias.

The era was not uneventful, however. The "Comunidades" (people's uprisings) at the start of Carlos I reign is one example. The Castillian rebels, called "comuneros", protesting against the new monarchy's practice of dividing out the choice positions to foreigners and their entourages who arrived for the sole purpose of making enough money to finance their claims to become emperor of some distant land, asked for the support of Seville. The Seville Council decided to stay loyal to the monarchy and declined participation in the rebellion. Only a few nobles led by Don Juan de Figueroa, the brother of the Duke of Arcos, took up the ambiguous rebel call of "Long live the King and the Comunidad". A total of seven hundred men equipped with artillery belonging to Duke of Arcos descended on the Plaza de San Francisco.

The house of Medina Sidonia, having, from the first, sworn allegiance to the King, put together a small squadron and managed to force the rebels to retreat towards the Alcazar. The Seville authorities appealed to the citizens to help put down the rebellion, but when they arrived in the vicinity of the Alcazar they found that Medina Sidonia's troops had already forced the rebels to disband. Their were some deaths in the skirmishes and prisoners taken were executed shortly afterwards.

The Emperor showed his undying gratitude for Seville's loyalty by celebrating his marriage to Isabel of Portugal there.

The ceremony took place on the 11th of March 1526 and celebrations were to be remembered for a long time to come. The

Towards the end of the XVII century the Merchants Exchange was built alongside the cathedral, the work of the architect Herrera. Today it houses the General Archive of the Indies.

welcome extended to the Royal Couple, with huge triumphal arches and enormous crowds, would be remebered for a long time to come. Isabel arrived eight days before her groom, who entered the city through la Macarena and proceeded to the cathedral where he stopped to pray into front of Nuestra Señora de la Antigua, before going on to the Alcazar where the future Queen was already in residence. According to chroniclers of the time, they were married that night by the Archbishop of Toledo. A banquet was held afterwards attended by the entourages of both parties. Amid the dancing and fireworks and other festivities the party soon reached dawn.

The Kings stayed another two months in Seville amusing themselves with the jousts and tournaments, the bullfights and the "juegos de cañas" (a mock war game played on horseback with canes instead of lances) that took place in the Plaza de San Fransisco. From what the chronicler Ortiz de Zuñiga has written, the Easter celebrations of that year were more festive and splendid than ever before.

It was not all happiness in the city in those times. There were often catastrophes, the most feared of which was the flooding of the river. More than ten floods were to leave their tragic mark on the city in the sixteenth century alone. The bridge of barges linking Seville to the Triana area was carried away several times, and hundreds of houses were destroyed each time the river broke its banks. The almost continual damage to the El Arenal zone, used as a storage area for goods bound for the New World, caused severe losses in the commercial sector.

The heavy rains which fell in 1626 raised the water level to the point of inundating every village in the Guadalquivir valley. Contemporary accounts claim that water reached the cathedral steps, submerged houses and inflicted material damage calculated at four million ducados.

Epidemics normally came in the wake of catastrophy. Germs grew in the warm, humid conditions and there was very little that could be done to stop them spreading. The only remedy known, the burning of clothes and belongings of the deceased, was not sufficient to stop the spreading of the epidemic.

Mention has already been made of the terrible 1649 plague but there were in fact two other extremely serious ones, in 1601 and 1680.

The devastation caused by the plague was greater in the 1600's due to conditions generated by the economic collapse and the slump in industrial and mercantile trade.

The days of the Golden Age now seemed a long way away, and the poverty and misery of the mid-seventeenth century was surely the reason for the 1652 uprising. The "Motin de la Feria" (Feria mutiny) –so called because its strongest redoubt was in the neighborhood of that name– held the future of Seville in balance for the whole of the month of May.

The monetary policy of Felipe IV's government was the spark that set off the conflict. In 1651 the goverment changed the value of the currency to such an extent that the citizens were left without purchasing power. The effect was to send prices spiralling and consumers to react with indignation.

The Giraldillo statue, which gave the Giralda Tower its name.

Disturbances broke out in various Andalusian cities and in Seville the crowds rose to the cry "Long live the King and death to the bad government!" Houses, where it was suspected wheat was stored for speculation purposes, were searched and some businesses stormed. In Triana, four thousand men joined the uprising.

A Sevillian nobleman, Don Juan de Villasis, who had a certain following amongst the people, was appointed by the council to persuade the rebels, now strongly entrenched in the la Feria area, to abandon their cause. It was the use of force which was to prove decisive, however. The offensive, using the tactics of speed and surprise, met hardly any resistance and the instigators of the revolt were duly captured and condemned.

This episode in Seville's history ends with a note of desperation among its inhabitants, frustrated by Felipe IV's misguided policies which were actually accentuating the crisis that already existed.

In spite of negative circumstances, Seville continued to be a friendly city and was improved in this era by new buildings and an urban style which changed its physiognomy. The calle Geneva, one of the streets widened, in time became the principle artery of the city, whose centre was moving towards the river. New squares and open spaces were built, especially in front of the churches, with an abundance of statues and ornamental gardens.

The second half of the sixteenth century saw the culmination of the project by the architect Hernan Ruiz to put the finishing touches to the old turret of the mosque with a series of bells crowned by a revolving statue acting as weathervane. This "Giraldillo" (weathervane) representing both Faith and Victory gave the tower its name –La Giralda.

The riches flowing in from the Americas encouraged the creation of magnificent works of art which have survived to this day. During those years the city became a focal point for architects, painters, sculptors and all kinds of artists drawn there in search of commissions or the patronage of institutions or individuals with wealth to spare.

A number of top ranking artists, with a style very much their own but with universal appeal, appeared on the scene. Names like Diego Velazquez, Bartolome Murillo, and Valdes Leal give some idea of the importance of Seville art in the Baroque period.

CHAPTER VII

THE SEVILLE OF THE ENLIGHTENMENT

Nostalgia for the Golden Age

The turn of the eighteenth century was to mark a change in the course of Seville's history; a change very much related to the loss of the leading role to which, under the Austrias, it had become so accustomed, and the new circumstances brought by the Bourbon dynasty in Spain.

Throughout eighteenth century Seville was to try, in vain, to recuperate the power –based on the commercial monopoly of trade with the New World– it had held a hundred years before. The exclusivity had been gradually whittled away until finally, in 1717, the Casa de Contratacion was moved to its new site in Cadiz.

Efforts to solve the crisis were shackled by a backward looking approach. Eighteenth century Seville was in a state of almost constant nostalgia for its recent past, something that would present difficulties when the time came to devise realistic strategies for the future. Seville fell victim to a profound parochialism, and in the 18th century it became a city of introspection and limited horizons.

As in the rest of Spain there were confrontations between the traditionalists and the innovators who, though fewer in number, made efforts to lift the city out of the stagnancy into which it had fallen. The 1700's, and especially the latter half, were key years in Seville's history. Here, its new role both at regional and national level was being outlined. Though it would keep trade with the Americas very much in mind, it would not be the linchpin of its existence.

Seville and the new Dynasty

After the death of the last monarch of the House of Austria, Seville did not hestitate in choosing sides in the battle for succession. Within a few days of the death of Carlos II who left no heir, the Seville Council met in extraordinary session to recognize Felipe of Anjou as the legitimate successor over the other candidate, Archduke Charles of Austria.

Seville was to prove a staunch supporter of Felipe when it came to providing funds and soldiers for the War of Succession which divided Spain and the most important European countries. Though no battle was fought on its soil, Felipe's every victory was greeted in Seville with jubilation and thanksgiving masses. In recognition, Felipe maintained Seville's exemptions and privileges and publicly recognized the loyaly which the city had demonstrated.

Relations between the new Bourbon King and Seville became even closer when he decided to take up residence in the city in 1729. Seville had already become accustomed to Royal visits, whether for festive reasons like the wedding of Carlos I, or for economic and political reasons as was the case with Felipe II and Felipe IV. Felip V, however, had no clear reason for establishing his Court in Seville, other than that the city offered the right climate and tranquility for the restoration of his deteriorating health.

During his five year stay in the city the King amused himself on the numerous hunts that were organized on estates near the city, such as La Corchuela and Monte Quintos. The knights gave demonstrations of their equestrian skills in El Patio de Banderas and there were "cañas" and bullfights –though the Royal Family were not particularly fond of the latter. During the King's stay in the city the remains of Saint Fernando were moved to a new tomb to facilitate veneration by the faithful.

The remains of the Saint can still be seen in the Royal chapel of Seville cathedral.

The transfer of the Court to Seville did present some problems, however. There were enormous costs involved in smartening up the city, in the gifts and donations offered by the town council and in the preparation of lodgings for the vast royal entourage.

Seville would have to wait until the end of the century to receive another royal visit. In 1796 Carlos IV spent eleven days with his family in the city for the purpose of kneeling down in front of the body of Saint Fernando to offer thanks for the recovery from a malignant illness of the heir to the throne, the future Fernando VII. There were celebrations and festive events of every type, though this time the brevity of the visit did not weigh so heavily on the city's purse.

Society and Economy in the Eighteenth Century

The population of Seville, which had dropped considerably during the seventeenth century to a low of 60,000 at the outset of Felipe V's reign, began to gradually increase, reaching a figure of 80,000 in the last quarter of the century.

The social structure of the city did not undergo any significant changes since the days of the Austrias. The different social classes were affected to a greater or lesser extent by the changes which had taken place throughout Spain, and especially in Seville, where wealth and prosperity had contributed to reduce class differences. From 1700 on, rampant parochialism again accentuated those differences which, though they had not ceased to exist, had, nevertheless, not been so apparent.

The nobility saw its numbers reduced by the exodus of some of some greatest families like the Osuna and Medinaceli to Madrid. The power of the nobles as a group was not significantly altered, however. They still maintained similar social status, wealth and monopoly of municipal power and, if anything, increased that power thanks to the granting of new titles. The Galindo and Aguila Houses were made Counts and the Villamarin, Marquesses.

The Real Maestranza de Caballeria (Royal Equestrian Society of Knights), a body which aimed to emulate, at a regional level, the Courtly nobility, grew considerably in this period. The Maestranza of Seville had been founded in 1670 but Felipe V granted it a series of privileges and its first statutes. It was headed by a President who had always to be one of the King's sons. Members were under special jurisdiction and had their own uniform, an imitation of that used by officials in the Kings regiment. In 1733 the Maestranza obtained permission to build the bullring in Baratillo which still exists, albeit considerably modified.

Fransisco Aguilar Piñal, a scholar of the period, maintains that there were 15,830 people in the service of the Church in Seville in the mid-eighteenth century. There were large differences, though, between the upper and lower clergy.

The Seville prelates continued to share out their substantial rents with generosity and liberality. A good example was Archbishop Arias (1701-1717) who, on the pretext of Philip V's victories in Italy, ordered the sharing out of his rental income among the convents, hospitals and poor of the city.

The lower clergy lived with very few means, while the regular clergy lived under very diverse conditions. The most numerous of the latter were the Fransiscans, followed by the Mercedarians, the Dominicans and the Carmelites. In the reign of Carlos III efforts were made to develop the work of the parishes with the intention of using them as instruments of Bourbon reformism. The men of the Enlightenment took a different attitude to the regular clergy whom they considered useless and burdensome to the public. Jovellanos thought the nuns "should be forced to do knitting", and Pablo de Olvide considered that numerous monks and nuns in Seville lived "from the sweat of the poor". As a consequence of Carlos III's policy of cutting the influence and power held by some religious orders in society, the Jesuits were expelled in 1767. Their wealth was seized by the Crown and used to defray costs resulting from school and hospital reform.

The majority of people in Seville who were neither nobles nor clergy worked as administrators, artisans, day labourers and salaried workers. The working population was made up of approximately 32,000 people, the majority of whom were members of the rigid guilds system. Weavers, potters, carpenters and bakers amongst others were dotted around the city, each according to his trade; the potters could be found in the Triana barrio, while transport workers were grouped in the Magdalena area. Brotherhoods had already begun to flourish in the sixteenth century under the umbrella of the guilds. Many of them became religious groups giving penance for the death of Christ and organizing processions with images of the Passion. Easter, as we now know it, has its roots in this period and was a major event in the eighteenth century.

With the switch to Cadiz as base for mercantile trade with the Americas and the economic downturn that followed, the number of foreigners in Seville dropped considerably. The Moors had already vanished from the Seville scene and there were very few slaves left. The "Gitanos" (gypsies) were the only minority who survived, in spite of Bourbon efforts to integrate them with the rest of the populace. During Carlos III's reign Seville's gitanos, some of whom worked in the tobacco factory, numbered about two thousand.

Of all sectors of the economy hit by the loss of the monopoly with the Indies, it was the agricultural one that was hit the hardest. Already in the second half of the seventeenth century a significant drop had been registered in exports of fruit to the other side of the Atlantic, and the eighteenth century was to see this trend accentuated. There were no major innovations in agricultural techniques and no significant changes in the system of land ownership. The nobility still held on to the vast majority of Seville's land. Towards the end of the century a shift did occur, however, with the change from long leases to short leases of an average of five years for municipal land sold to satisfy the demand from peasant smallholders. It was timed to coincide with the freedom of the Corn Trade in 1765. This measure, a gesture on the Governments part to alleviate the conditions of the peasantry, had the immediate effect of raising prices. In the longer term it brought greater profits, caused a revaluation of the land and an increase in production.

In the eighteenth century industry continued to be a sector of secondary importance. The biggest industries were state sponsored rather than in private hands. The Tobacco Factory was, without doubt, the most important enterprise. Though founded in the seventeenth century, it was only in the eighteenth that it began to flourish –to such an extent that a new factory was built near the Puerta de Jerez and went into production in 1758. Nowadays, the building is occupied by some of the faculties and offices of the University of Seville. The facade and a few of the patios still testify to its previous use.

Other state enterprises were the Royal Artillery Works which moved into what had been the Royal Dockyards, in 1719, its three furnaces producing high quality parts; "la Real Fábrica de Salitre" (Royal Saltpetre Factory), and the Real Almacén de Maderas del Segura (Royal Wood Warehouse) which commercialized the wood sent downriver to Seville from the Sierra del Segura.

Other artesanal activities were very much controlled by the rules of their powerful guilds, so powerful in fact that they acted as a brake on the productive process. The textile industry was the most active producing cotton, silk and wool products. Its development was encouraged by the "Economic Society of Friends of the Country", established in 1775, and dedicated to the training of personnel and the introduction of new techniques.

The Bourbon policy of developing industry and commerce with the Americas, together with traders anxious not to lose the economic links already developed, led to to the creation of the Real Companía de San Fernando in 1747. The company's aim was to produce textile products for export to the other side of the Atlantic. Its main shareholders were Flemish merchants and during the first few years of its life it employed large numbers of people. Low profits and hostility from the merchants of Cadiz, angry at the extent of state benefits the company received, forced its closure. By 1778 the company had ceased to exist.

Period engraving of the main facade of the Tobacco Factory, XVIII century.

The Seville of the City Official Olavide

The Bourbons carried out important reforms to municipal administration, one of which was the creation of the post of "Intendente". It was modelled on the French Louis XIV's system and had police, legal and military reponsibilities. The Intendente eventually evolved into a Governor of the province and Corregidor of the capital he chose to set up his headquarters in.

In Seville, the Asistente had been the highest power and, now, in addition to his traditional roles were added those of Superintendant General of Incomes and Superintendant General of the Army. Seville's Asistente was therefore not only a mayor but had a series of powers transcending the purely local.

There were some good Asistentes in Seville at this time. Don Ramon de Larumbe (1760-1767), for example, was responsible for organizing important public works. The most famous of all, however, was Pablo de Olavide, a man with remarkable perso-

SE

PRADO DE SAN

PLANO TOPOGRAPHICO
de la
M.N.Y.M.L.CIUDAD
de Sevilla.

SE LEVANTÒ, Y ABRIÒ
POR DISPOSICION DEL
Sr. D. PABLO DE OLA
VIDE. ASISTENTE DE
ESTA CIUDAD, INTEN
DENTE DEL EXERCI-
TO, Y PROVINCIA DE
ANDALUCIA. Y SUPE-
RINTENDENTE DE
LAS NUEVAS POBLA
CIONES DE SIERRA-
MORENA, Y ANDALU-
CIA. AÑO DE 1771.
Escala de 600 Varas Castellanas
Se publica a iniciativa y expensas del Instituto de Estudios Sevillanos.

Olavide's plan, XVIII century.

nality and untiring energy, who promoted numerous social, economic and cultural enterprises. Olavide, born in Lima, Peru in 1725, rose to the position of judge. For economic motives he left his home city, arriving in Spain in 1752, where he came under the wing of the Count of Aranda. The Spanish politician used his influence to get him nominated Intendente of the four kingdoms of Andalusia and Asistente of Seville.

Olavide did a lot for the city. He organized the tax system, encouraged agriculture, introduced an efficient street cleaning system, regulated the functioning of the food markets, and cleaned up and restored the riverside Laguna area, with new streets and houses and general redevelopment of a zone which hitherto had been disease and crime ridden.

On the basis of a topographical map which he had commissioned, Olavide divided the city into four districts, and then those districts into eight "barrios". Streets and buildings were adorned with ornate glazed tile signs, some of which can still be seen today.

During his stay in Seville, Olavide took up residence in the palace of the Alcazar and hosted a series of literary and musical events attended by the leading Seville intellectuals of the day, and the odd personality who happened to be passing through the city. He encouraged the Academies and dedicated a lot of attention to teaching. His proposed reform of university education met fierce opposition from some religious orders who saw their interests in jeopardy. The protests succeeded in attracting the attention of the Holy Office (the Inquisition) and the Asistente was called to Madrid in 1775, tried, and condemned to eight years in prison.

Meanwhile in the city, floods continued to wreak their periodic havoc, and the earthquake of 1775 damaged many monuments and destroyed hundreds of dwellings. There had been some improvements though.

The Paseo de Arenal was opened in the first years of the century, and in 1729 the Cruz del Campo road which ran from the the San Benito monastery to the Humilladero was improved. The "Torre de Oro" (Tower of Gold) was restored in 1760 and finished with small castles in the upper part. Many churches were built and restoration of existing ones carried out. At the end of the century the houses of the old Los Olmos enclosure were demolished and the Plaza de la Virgen de los Reyes built. The San Telmo palace, started in 1682, was finally finished and became the new site for the Navegation College and the Tobacco Factory.

During Carlos III's reign the "Casa Lonja" was converted into the Archive of the Indies –henceforth to store all the documentation relating to the Latin American colonies previously stored in the Simancas Archive.

The prohibition of bullfighting in Spain in 1754 stopped work on the Real Maestranza's bullring, not to restart until the lifting of the ban five years later. The change from mounted to standing bullfighters that took place about this time perhaps accounts for the extraordinary popularity of some bullfighters. The rivalry between the matadors Pepe-Hillo Costillares and Pedro Romero was the topic of conversation in every bar in Seville. The theatre was the other public spectacle of Seville.

Performances of certain works met opposition from the most conservative sectors on the grounds of morality. One of Olavide's first actions was to back the theatre. Performances were more carefully organized, a drama school was set up and grants awarded to theatrical companies. A theatre was built in the Plaza del Duque to supplement the only other one, a wooden structured building in the calle de San Eloy. In 1794 a new theatre, with a capacity of two thousand was built in the calle de la Muela. This may give some idea of the popularity of the theatre in these times. Perhaps it will also cause the reader to ponder on a society which found itself capable of sending a man of the calibre of Olvide to prison for eight years.

Between the arrival of the Bourbons and the Napoleonic invasion, Seville passed through a process of readaptation where the bases of what the city would be in the contemporary era were laid. It was a city coming to terms with its glorious past and the more minor role it was to play in the future.

The Giralda. "The Illustrated London News."

CHAPTER VIII

ROMANTIC AND LIBERAL SEVILLE

Seville in the War of Independence

The War of Independence, where the Spanish fought to rid the country of Napoleonic troops, marks the beginning of the contemporary era in Spain. But 1808 would also be remebered as the year when huge fissures were to split the political, social and economic system of the Old Regime and culminate in the triumph of the Liberal Revolution.

Events of vital importance for Spain were to take place in Seville.

The French revolution was followed with great interest in Seville, in spite of the authorities' attempts to censure news in the fear of similar events ocurring. In a series of diplomatic about-turns Carlos IV and his minister Godoy swopped fear for alliance with the neighbouring country in 1795. Such manoevering was to cost the Spanish King his throne. Opposition was brought to a head in the Aranjuez uprising which forced the removal of Carlos IV and the proclamation of his son, Ferdinand VII King. The crowning of the new King coincided, however, with the occupation of the country by its supposed allies from the other side of the Pyrenees.

The May 2 uprising against the prescence of Napoleon's troops in Madrid was followed by the formation of War Councils throughout the peninsula. In Seville, a Supreme Junta of Spain and the Indies was set up on the 27th of May, presided over by Fransisco Saavedra, using a part of the Alcazar palace as base of operations. To better coordinate resistance to the French, this Junta merged with others around the country to form the Central Supreme Junta. The advance of Napolean's troops forced the Central Junta to move south to Seville where it remained for several months, before surrendering to General Victor on the Ist of February 1810. From then until 1812 Seville was ruled by Joseph I Bonaparte, brother of Napolean and now King of Spain.

The French were to make significant changes to Seville during their two year occupation. The Agustinas Recoletas de la Encarnación monastery was demolished and a central market built in its place. The modernizing flair of the new authorities should not let us forget, however, the abuses committed by the French, especially with regard to the city's artistic heritage. Many paintings and objects of art were taken out of churches and other public buildings and brought over the hills to France.

From the summer of 1812 the French troops began to retreat, pressurized on one front by the Duke of Wellington's troops and on the other by Eastern Europe. On the 15th of August troops began to be evacuated together with Joseph's administrative apparatus. Allied troops made up of Spanish, Portuguese and English contingents entered the city on the 27th of August to the jubilation of the people of Seville.

Fernando VII's reign

After the liberation of the city, the Sevillians proclaimed the 1812 Constitution drawn up and approved by the Juntas in Cadiz during the war. A provisional Government, headed by Joaquin Goyeneta, was appointed but forced to disband after a short time. Absolute monarchy was reestablished and the Cadiz Accords rescinded following the return of Fernando VII to Spain.

The first years of Fernando's reign were fraught with difficulties for Seville, as a result of the precarious state of local authority finance and the economy in general. The Liberal Revolution of 1820 brought no effective solutions to problems aggravated by independence fever in the colonies.

The "Emancipation" had an extraordinary effect on Seville. One might have expected that having already lost the monopoly, the economy would not be too adversely affected. This was not so, however. The independance of the colonies plunged the economy into a new crisis and dampened the enthusiasm for recuperation so evident in eighteenth century Seville.

Still, the final stage of Fernando VII's reign, the so-called *Ominous Decade*, did have its positive side, especially as regards local authority politics. The Asistente Jose Manuel de Arjona brought about changes to the running of the Council. There were improvements in town planning with completion of new "paseos" –El Duque, las Delicias and Cristina. In the city centre, new iron street lamps were installed, and the main streets cobbled and paved. Access routes from Cruz del Campo and Triana were improved and the supply of produce guaranteed by skilful control of the markets. A new water supply system was built and special attention given to the control of public order.

In the cultural area, Arjona reestablished and raised the status of the School of Noble Arts, founded the Bullfighting Academy, promoted the Conservatory of Dramatic Art, and financed the publication of wide-ranging periodicals.

On balance, in the first third of the nineteenth century, in spite the political ups and downs and the catastrophe caused by the War of Independence, no event really altered the historical trajectory of Seville. The Liberal Revolution was for Seville, and indeed for the rest of the country, a paper revolution with no real and lasting effect until the death of Ferdinand VII.

The era of Isabel II

This era begins with the Regency of Maria Cristina, Isabel being too young to ascend to the throne. Despite the temporary nature of the Regency, the country lived through an intense period of transition whose effects were to be felt in Seville.

Seville changed from kingdom to province in 1833 as a result of the reforms prepared by the Minister of Development Javier de Burgos. Although still holding on to its capital status, the territory under its jurisdiction was significantly reduced. Land which for centuries had had Seville as its political and administrative centre was now outside its provincial area. The expropriation of ecclesiastical properties, prepared by the Minister Mendizabal in 1836, had important ramifications for Seville's economic and social development. Religious orders, except for those of public beneficence, were abolished by a series of decrees and their property taken over by the State. The confiscated properties then went under the auctioneer's hammer. Though the reasons were fundamentally economic –the State was on the verge of bankruptcy– the consecuences of this measure were to extend far beyond the purely financial.

In Seville, the expropriation of ecclesiastical property was considerable. Confiscated goods and property made up a quarter of the total for the whole of Andalusia. The result was to reinforce the tendancy to "Latifundism" –the creation of even bigger estates.

Another important disentailment was carried out in 1855 and basically affected local authority property. The bill was prepared by the Minister Pascual de Madoz and it affected Seville very much like the ecclesiastical disentailment. The nobles and the bourgoisie took up the new opportunity to add to their already sizeable estates and, in so doing, exacerbated tensions between themselves and the dispossessed. The Seville countryside was the scene of numerous peasant uprisings in this century.

The nobility had proved capable of weathering the revolutionary storm and, indeed, of taking advantage of it. Although they lost the privileges they had had under the Old Regime, their wealth remained intact during Isabel's reign. Their ranks were swelled by the new middle class landowners, creating an aristocracy that was to maintain its hold over the rest of society through its not inconsiderable economic and political power.

The guilds had disappeared from Seville in Fernando VII's time. What became of the numerous artisans with their diverse crafts of days gone by? Seville did not have the industrial infrastructure to absorb the surplus labour which in other cities had been thrown onto the capitalist market to there suffer the abuses of the system. Many artisans did continue to practice their skills, though now under conditions of free competition and without the protection they had hitherto enjoyed under the union.

The clergy in Seville suffered the effects of the disentailment of the Church. It caused each member to suffer personally and impeded the maintenance of assistential, cultural and religious functions previously carried out by the now extinct religious orders. However, the reorganization of the diocese by Cardinal Romo during the middle of Isabel II's reign, in accord with the directives of the 1851 Concordat, encouraged the Church to adapt to the new situation.

The population of Seville rose considerably over the course of this period. The 1857 census listed 120,000 people –a figure which was to grow steadily to 150,000 by the end of the century.

Economically, however, Seville was unable to recover. The end of the colonies in the Americas left the city as a mere regional commercial centre. The few business initiatives –a tanning factory, a metalurgical plant and a ceramics factory (Wetherell & Pickman)– were in the hands of foreigners. These foreign enterprises did, however, provide a lead to the native population, and some industrial development did take place. But there were huge problems in attracting investment from the native bourgoisie, more interested in putting their money into land than into factories.

In 1846, it was surprisingly a Catalan, Narciso Bonaplata and a Basque, Jose Maria de Ibarra, who were the driving force behind the creation of what would later be one of Seville's special traditions: the April fair. What was to begin as a mainly agricultural fair would later become the stage for celebrating the culture unique to Seville; its dances and its its music and its bullfighters etc.

The Bank of Seville, founded in 1856, soon ran into financial trouble and the economic crisis of 1866 was severe enough to deal it the final blow. Communications improved mainly as a result of the railway. The Seville-Cordoba line was opened in 1859, the Seville-Cadiz line a year later and the transversal Utrera-Morón in 1864. The Isabel II bridge over the Guadalquivir was also built in this period.

The Isabel period was also the Romantic period. It was here that the rather mythical, deformed and superficial image of Seville was created, many of whose facets have survived up to the present day. The figure of the immortal Don Juan Tenorio, created by Jose Zorrilla, or *Rhymes and Legends* by Gustavo Adolfo Becquer –the most popular Sevillian poet of all time– were the points of reference for the definition of Romantic Seville. Visitors to Seville from abroad in the first half of the century were also responsible for the creation of this image. For them Seville represented the quintessence of the whole nation. The bullfighter, the woman cigarette maker and the bandit, supposedly so characteristic of the area, would often be considered as Spanish architypes. Seville became a city glorified in literature, recited by poets and the setting of several operas composed in this period.

From Revolution to Restoration

Seville became involved in the revolution which erupted in September 1868 and which toppled Isabel from the throne. From the San Telmo palace in Seville, the Duke of Montpensier, husband of princess Luisa Fernanda and, as such, brother-in-law of the Queen, conspired openly with rebel generals. His triumph opened the way for a period of six unstable years in the country.

The revolutionary fervour of the most agitated sections in Seville provoked a series of riots. Numerous buildings were damaged and various churches set on fire. The federalist republicans of Seville, small in number though they were, played an important part in the revolutionary process. Once the new Constitution came into effect in 1869 and the democratic monarchy of D. Amadeo de Saboya established, there was a lull in the revolutionary activity so characteristic of the sixties.

The Duke of Montpensier's claim to the throne was dismissed both for his part in the federal uprising in Seville and for killing Enrique de Borbón in a duel. A significant part of the aristocracy embraced the Carlist cause, then beginning to find support in the city.

Amadeus I, failing in his attempts to bring agreement to the different parties in the constitutional power struggle, was forced to abdicate in 1873, after only two years on the throne. The First Spanish Republic was proclaimed immediately afterwards.

There was a tide of republican fervour in Seville and now, with the proclamation of the new political regime, the disinherited classes glimpsed the possibilty of a redistribution through social upheaval. There were strikes in the construction, iron and weaving industriess and the Republican Militia siezed the arms stored in the Maestranza de Artillería (Arsenal). The Seville Canton was proclaimed on the 19th of July. Decrees issued during the few days that it lasted reduced the working day to eight hours, established the right to work as a part of the right to live, and granted the right to resolve labour disputes by agreement between the two parties involved, without exterior interference.

The Canton revolt pushed the Republic to the right and General Pavia was ordered to crush the fragmentary movement. Pavia and his soldiers entered Seville on the 30th of July and in the resulting clash with the Militias there were considerable number of deaths and material damage.

The failure of federal republicanism dragged the republican regime down with it. After a provisional government was installed under General Serrano and as everything possible had been tried, the logical thing to do was to go back to scratch. The Bourbon monarchy was thus restored in the person of Alfonso XII, the son of the Queen dethroned in 1868.

Alfonso XII was crowned King on 29 December 1874 after a pronouncement by General Martinez Campos in Sagunta. Political stability combined with economic recovery. Factories were built to process agricultural produce mainly for export (flour, beer and cooking oil), and some chemical plants were constructed.

At the same time, a progressive decline in traditional sectors like textiles and metallurgy began to take place. Commerce continued to be the most important urban activity together with what we might call tertiary activities. Seville continued to attract country people seeking a more comfortable and dignified life. The majority of servants and cheap labour were drawn from their ranks, and they were to make up a significant portion of the membership of the workers movements springing up to channel the protests of the discontented.

Urbanistically, this first stage of the Restoration was not to prove very positive for the city. Some attempts were made to to construct low cost housing on the outskirts –to cater for the severe problems of overcrowding and disease in which many Sevillians lived. These projects were frustrated by the shortsightedness of local authority politicians, and the egotism of the dominant social groups.

The donation of the San Telmo gardens to the public by the Dukes of Montpensier –who had returned to Seville as a result of the restoration of the Bourbons to the throne– was of great importance for the city.

As regards public works, in 1882 an English company was given the contract to convert the water supply, street lighting was further improved and more ships visited Seville as a result of dock improvements. It was an era when some of the aspects of city life were modernized; the telephone was introduced and the horse-drawn trams were changed to electrically powered with the advent of electricity in 1887.

While the nineteenth century closed with an atmosphere of political stability in spite of huge social desequilibriums and a weak economy, Seville continued to dream about becoming the great metropolis of the south.

CHAPTER IX

SEVILLE BETWEEN EXPO'29 AND EXPO'92

Seville in the early 20th Century

From whatever perspective the history of Seville in the first three decades of this century is considered, the Ibero-American Exhibition of 1929 will always appear as the key event around which others revolve.

"Catalyser of forces", "Most important undertaking carried out by the Seville city council", or "Motor of the changes in Seville in the 20th century", have been some of the comments used to describe this historic event.

The Exhibition appeared to the people of Seville as the spur to the definitive recovery that they had been demanding since the 17th century. Furthermore, the fact that the Exhibition was Ibero-American led to hopes of renewing those relations with the Americas which had been so important for the development of the city.

Seville was in great need of some stimulus to lift it from the state of inertia into which it had fallen. Its economic and social position at the turn of the century was nothing short of pitiable. In real terms the population was declining with a higher death rate than birth rate. Indeed, the death rate was one of the highest in Europe at that time. The figures were to some extent bolstered up by the influx of people from the country. Between 1900 and 1920 the population of Seville had risen by thirty per cent to a figure of 205,000 inhabitants.

The problem was that the population growth was made up, in the main part, by an uprooted people with few resources and living under terrible conditions. At this time it was possible to draw a dividing line across the city with the well-off south on one side and the industrial, artesan, proletarian north on the other. In the latter, the people lived in blocks of flats and "corralas" (tiny flats with outside tolets) in appalling conditions. Still worse were the conditions of those forced to live in "chabolas" (makeshift huts). Construction of living space was way below the level needed to house a population with few economic resources.

Businesses were unable to absorb the masses of labourers now flooding into the city. Only a little over a third of the inhabitants could consider themselves employed and, of those, the vast majority were salaried employees.

The Ibero-American Exhibition transformed the city both in the urban and the economic sense. The demand for labour solved the employment problems of many Sevillians and connections with the Americas renewed.

The mid nineteenth century was the era of great exhibitions –London (1862), Vienna (1873), Philadelphia (1876), Paris (1878), Barcelona(1888)– which publicised the production, commerce, culture and art of the participating countries.

The idea of holding an exhibition of this type was first mooted in 1909, as the regenerative initiative of a circle led by Luis Rodriguez Caso, a well known local employer, and supported by some local businessmen and traders.

At first it was no easy task convincing the Government of the suitability and viability of the project. Seville had the advantage of already being popular with tourists and thus capable of attracting visitors to the exhibition. Another factor was the enthusiasm of the people of Seville for hosting the exhibition. These, together with the appointment of the Liberal Antonio Halden as mayor in 1910, were sufficient reasons for the government to decide in favour of the city.

After surmounting innumerable difficulties and postponements, at last, in 1929, the Seville Ibero-American Exhibition was opened. The exhibition took place during the dictatorship

*Period engraving. An aspect of Seville in the latter half
of the XIX century.*

of Primo de Rivera who had come to power after a coup d'etat in 1923 in which the Constitution was temporarily suspended. The dictator became personally involved with the success of the exhibition and the appointment of Cruz Conde as commissioner of the same was decisive to the outcome.

The Exhibition was sited on land bordering the Parque de Maria Luisa in the southern part of the city. Pavilions were erected for each of the Ibero-American countries represented and for other countries and institutions wishing to participate. Some of the most outstanding, such as those of Argentina, Peru, Mexico, Guatemala and Chile are still conserved, some in a better state than others. Other buildings such as the Plaza de España, the Lope de Vega theatre and the Alfonso XII hotel would complete the architectural preparations.

A series of urban developments would turn Seville into what it is more or less today. The avenidas de Eduardo Dato, de la Borbolla, Reina Mercedes and La Palmera were opened; the Santa Cruz district and the area around the Archivo de Indias was redeveloped and the San Bernardo bridge completed; all of which greatly facilitated the city's expansion.

While the Exhibition provided a much needed impetus for the modernization of Seville, from the economic point of view it was disastrous. Unfortunately, this was also the year of the world-wide slump which significantly reduced the number of visitors and the city council, having taken the financial weight of the enterprise, faced bankruptcy.

Social tensions, kept at bay by the demand for labour for the exhibition, resurfaced even more violently once the exhibition had closed its doors.

The fall of the dictatorship in the early thirties, followed by the fall of Alfonso XIII, and the proclamation of the Second Republic, opened a new cycle in the dynamic history of Spain and Seville.

The Republic and the Civil War

The Republican regime proclaimed in April 1931 was to suffer the effects of the general crisis. The city received the name "Sevilla la roja" (Red Seville) because of the extent of worker affiliation to the anarchist union (CNT), the socialist (UGT) and the various communist unions.

Electorally, the Republicans, led by Diego Martinez Barrios, and the Socialists captured 60 per cent of the votes, leaving the Monarchists with only 25 per cent. The Republican-Socialist alliance faced fierce opposition from the left (anarchists and communists) who were organizing strikes and disturbances, and conspiracy from the right which culminated in the the August 10 coup, led by General Sanjuro. This created a problem of public order and an unprecedented level of street violence culminating in the assassination of one of the leading employers, Pedro Caravaca, on May 20 1933.

The elections of 1933 were won by the right after socialists and republicans decided to abandon their alliance. The conservatives were united in the group C.E.D.A. and divisions within the coalition government until then, permitted the establishment of a Radical-Ceda Government.

In Seville, the new Government's policies were chiefly aimed at reversing the policies of its predecessor. Secular education was suspended and street names changed. What best reflected the change in Seville was the recommencement of religious processions at Easter time, interrupted for two years during the Republic.

However, despite the political and social changes, the people of Seville did their best to continue with their daily lives. There was still an animated atmosphere in the paseo de la Alameda and the parque de Maria Luisa; in the meetings and get-togethers which continued on the terraces of bars ande "tabernas" of popular districts, all of which perhaps expressed a desire to escape the problems which faced every level of society during those years.

The same might be said for the traditional "fiestas" which began to regain their popularity. The fair recovered its splendour, and the traditional Corpus procession, limited under the Republic to the Cathedral grounds, was able to file through the city and to enjoy official representation from the Seville city council.

Football began to grow in popularity particularily when two Sevillian clubs were promoted to the First Division; first Betis in 1932, and Seville F.C two years later.

As regards bullfighting, the legendary bullfighter Juan Belmonte made a reappearance in 1934, but to judge from contemporary accounts the years of the Republic were not especially good ones for the spectacle –both in the quality of matadors and in public attendance. A new bullring, the Monumental, inaugurated in 1918, was closed and later demolished due to declining gates.

The 1936 elections, won by the Popular Front, were seen by the left as reason to "liberate" the Republic of its enemies. The collaboration between reformist Republicans and worker's organizations became untenable. The latter wanted to resolve matters in the street. That winter, social and political conflicts reappeared and problems of violence and rioting were added to by the storms and floods which swept the city. Economic activities were in a state of paralysis and a climate of insecurity affected both rich and poor. This situation was to reach its climax in the tragic Civil War.

When the plot to overthrow the Republic was realized on 18 July, it fell to General Gonzalo Quiepo de Llano to bring Seville into the Francoist camp. He took over the city, quickly stifling the resistance offered by Civil Governor Jose Varela Rendueles and followers of the Republic.

The African army soon touched down at Tablada aerodrome –after a precarious airlift organized from military strongholds in Morrocco.

Once the supression of rebel forces had been consolidated, the city became a base from which General Fransisco Franco, who had set up headquarters in the Yanduri Palace, organized his first advances towards the north. When Franco left for the Castillian front, Quiepo stayed on in charge of Seville to make sure the city would act as a Franco rearguard throughout the Civil War. Amidst the setting up of makeshift hospitals –one was located inside the Exhibition centre– and the numerous

Aerial view of the Universal Exposition, "EXPO 92" with the city in the backround.

events that were being organized to raise war funds, time was still found for initiatives aimed at economically developing the city. The Fábrica de Hilados y Tejidores Andaluces, S.A. (Spinning and Weaving Factory) was built at this time and some urban projects realized.

Having backed the winner, Seville avoided many of the horrors of the war being suffered by other Spanish cities. Still, reprisals and "cleaning up operations" sent three thousand people to the firing squad and many others to prison. The ending of the Civil War in April 1939 marked the beginning of the long era of Franco's regime.

Seville from Franco to Democratic Monarchy

At the beginning of the forties, the people of Seville were urged to throw themselves to the task of national reconstruction, amidst an atmosphere of patriotic euphoria where General Franco appeared at the reigns of all the Spaniards who supported, or merely silently obeyed the new laws passed by his military regime.

These were hard years for the city with food shortages, restrictions in public services and the poverty so characteristic of a post-war country. Some solutions to age old problems were found, however. The Cartuja dam, inaugurated in 1949, finally put an end to the floods that had been an incessant headache to Sevilla throughout its history. The work consisted in diverting the course of the river behind the Triana fertile plain, in such a way that the waters ran into a closed dock in the Chapina area.

Other works like the construction of the Minilla reservoir for water supply to the city and the airport of San Pablo, attempted, not wholly successfully, to give Seville a more modern air. The lack of housing for the growing population, unemployment and the huge differences between different sectors in the city, gave rise to a feeling of sadness throughout the post-war years. Only the odd visit from some famous person would lift the city out of the monotony of its daily life. Eva Peron, who visited the city in June 1947, and the King of Saudi Arabia were both welcomed by huge crowds and celebrations. Even religiously, Seville had to suffer at the severe and strict hands of Cardenal D.Pedro Segura y Saenz who headed the Seville diocese until 1957.

The fifties were to see Spain emerging from the international isolation it had chosen since the end of the Second World War. This contributed to an economic recovery, especially in the first half of the sixties. Economic and social transformations were not accompanied by political changes. Franco's regime was not to ease its authoratarian hold one iota.

Of the three factors which accounted for the economic growth; foreign investment, emigration of workers and tourism, it was the latter two which had most effect on our city. A large part of the emigrant labour which went to Germany, Switzerland and other countries seeking opportunities they were unlikely to find in Spain, were from Seville. On the other hand Seville's fame as typically Spanish, its pintoresque quality and its historical heritages attracted some of the tourists now coming to Spain on a large scale. This tourism was but a passing affair, however, while more permanent sites were sought.

These years also witnessed the completion of the Los Remedios barrio, a fine example of the disastrous planning of the city authorities. There were positive steps though, like the improvement in access routes to the city with the opening of the dual carriageway at Dos Hermanos and the new stretch of motorway between Huelva and Castilleja de la Cuesta. The new Generalisimo bridge further facilitated comunications with the opposite bank of the Guadalquivir.

By the early seventies there were half a million inhabitants in Seville. The city seemed to have resigned itself to a more discreet role in national affairs. However, its appointment as capital of the Andalusian Autonomous Community, and later the concession of Expo 1992, raises hopes for the future of Seville.

The event is already helping to improve the urban infrastructure and communications of the city, exactly as it did in 1929. This Expo is dedicated to the Age of Discovery and more than a hundred countries and big companies will participate. The pavilions will occupy sites on the Isla de Cartuja, near to the Santa Maria de las Cuevas monastery. This major event has also inspired the building of the new Santa Justa railway station, a new terminal at San Pablo airport, and many other works certain to aid the development of Seville.

BIBLIOGRAPHY

Aguilar Piñal, Fransisco. *La Sevilla de Olavide*, Sevilla, Imprenta Municipal.

Aguilar Piñal, Fransisco. *Siglo XVIII*, from the collection *Historia de Sevilla*, Sevilla, publicaciones de la Universidad, 1989, (3rd ed.)

Blanco Freijero, Antonio. *La ciudad Antigua (De la prehistoria a los visigodos)*, from the collection *Historia de Sevilla*, Sevilla, Publicaciones de la Universidad 1989. (3rd Ed).

Bosch Vila, Jacinto. *La Sevilla Islamica*, from the collection *Historia de Sevilla*, Publicaciones de la Universidad, 1988 (2cd ed.)

Braojos, A., Parias, M. y Alvarez, L. *Sevilla en el siglo XX*, 2 vols. from the collection, *Historia de Sevilla*, Sevilla. Publicacions de la Universidad, 1990.

Chaunu, Pierre. *Sevilla y America. Siglos XVI y XVII*, Sevilla, Publicaciones de la Universidad, 1983.

Cuenca Toribio, Jose M. *Del Antiguo al Nuevo Regimen*, from the collection *Historia de Sevilla*, Sevilla, Publicaciones de la Universidad, 1988, (3rd ed.).

Dominguez Ortiz, Antonio. *Orto y Ocaso de Sevilla*, Sevilla, Publicaciones de la Universidad, 1974 (2cd ed.).

Domingo Ortiz, Antonio. *La Sevilla del Siglo XVII*, from the collection *Historia de Sevilla*, Sevilla, Publicaciones de la Universidad, 1989, (3rd ed.).

Guichot y Parody, Joaquin. *Historia de la ciudad de Sevilla y los pueblos importantes de la provincia de Sevilla*, Imprenta de Jimenez Orduña, 1873-1886.

Ladero Quesada, M.Angel. *La Ciudad Medieval (1248-1492)*, from the collection *Historia de Sevilla*, Sevilla, Publicaciones de la Universidad, 1989, (3rd ed.).

Morales Padron, Fransisco. *Sevilla Insolita*, Sevilla, Publicaciones de la Universidad, 1987, (5th ed.).

Morales Padron, Fransisco. *La ciudad del Quinientos*, from the collection *Historia de Sevilla*, Sevilla, Publicaciones de la Universidad, 1989, (3rd ed.).

VV.AA. *Sevilla en su provincia*, 4 vols. Sevilla, Ediciones Gever, 1983.

CHRONOLOGY

1000 BC   First settlements in Seville at around this date.

770 BC   Peak of Tartessan civilization. The Phoenicians establish themselves in Seville.

630 BC   Beginning of Argantonio's reign.

400 BC   The start of the Turdetan era.

230 BC   The Carthaginians in Seville.

206 BC   Battle of Ilipa. The Romans found Italica.

69 BC   Caesar in Seville.

61 BC   Caesar returns to Seville.

45 BC   Battle of Munda. Seville awarded the title *Colonia Iulia Romulo Hispalis*.

53 AD   Birth of Trajan.

76 AD   Birth of Hadrian.

250   First news of the organization of the Church in Seville.

380   Building of the first Christian Basilica (San Vicente Martir).

426   The arrival of the Vandals.

525   The Visigoths in Seville.

579   Hermenegild is proclaimed king.

589   Death of Saint Leandro, Bishop of Seville. His brother Saint Isidore succeeds him.

711   The Arabs arrive in Seville.

844   The Normans invade and sack Seville.

929   Abderraman III proclaims himself independant Caliph.

1039   Almutamid is born.

1086   Battle of Zalaca. The Almoravids rout Christian troops.

1091   Seville falls into Almoravid hands.

1147   The Almohades arrive in Seville.

1221   Construction of the Torre del Oro (Gold Tower).

1248   Reconquest of Seville by Fernando III the Saint.

1284   Death of Alfonso X the Wise.

1350   Pedro I the Cruel crowned King.

1391   Christians attack Jewish population.

1402   Work begins on the construction of the cathedral.

1481   The Inquisition Tribunal starts operating in Seville.

1492 The discovery of America. The Jewish community is expelled.
1502 Founding of the College of Santa Maria de Jesus, embryo of the future University of Seville.
1525 Wedding of the Emperor Carlos V to Isabel of Portugal in Seville's Alcazar.
1527 Construction begins on the Seville Council building.
1528 Termination of the building of the "Casa Lonja".
1623 The Conde Duque de Olivares grants the University of Seville special judicial status.
1649 Year of the great plague.
1652 The "Motin de la Feria" uprising.
1717 Transfer of the Casa de Contratacion to Cadiz.
1729 Felipe V moves the Court to Seville.
1747 The "Real Compania de San Fernando" is founded.
1747 Olavide is appointed "Asistente" of Seville.
1808 Creation in Seville of the "Junta Suprema de España e Indias" (Supreme Junta of Spain and the Indies).
1812 The exodus of Napoleonic troops from Seville.
1825 Jose M. de Arjona is appointed Asistente of Seville.
1833 Status of Seville changed from kingdom to province.
1836 Disentailment of the Church by Mendizabal.
1856 The Bank of Seville is created.
1857 The population of Seville reaches 150,000.
1859 Inauguration of the Seville-Cordoba railway line.
1873 Proclamation of the First Republic.
1887 Electriciy comes to Seville.
1929 Celebration of the Iberian-American Universal Exhibition.
1932 General Sanjurjo's rising in Seville on 10 August against the Republic.
1936 Franco sets up headquarters in the Yanduri palace.
1947 Eva Peron visits Seville.
1957 Cardinal Segura dies.
1961 Huge floods in Seville.
1975 Proclamation of Juan Carlos I as King of Spain.
1983 Seville is officially appointed host of Expo'92.